Making the most of your
Glorious
Glut

ACKNOWLEDGEMENTS

To Graham, Toby and Will for all their support and
encouragement and – together with the members of the
Abingdon Craft Club – for testing so many of the recipes.
Thanks particularly to Carole, whose bag of runner
beans gave me the idea for this book in the first place.

Making the most of your
Glorious
Glut

Cooking, storing, freezing, drying & preserving your garden produce

Jackie Sherman

green books

First published in 2011 by

Green Books,
Dartington Space, Dartington Hall,
Totnes, Devon TQ9 6EN

Photographs:
Jackie Sherman: pages 11, 47, 48, 50, 54, 61, 66, 73, 79, 81, 87, 93,
99, 101, 105, 109, 110, 113, 115, 116, 120, 125, 130, 132, 133, 135, 136, 148,
164, 166, 167, 168, 171, 173, 175, 188, 195, 198, 199, 214, 220, 227, 228,
230, 231, 237, 241, 243, back cover top left and top right.
Amanda Cuthbert: pages 23, 25, 27, 31, 39. Paul Hill: page 53.

Design by Jayne Jones
Illustrations by Ellie Mains

ISBN 978 1 900322 96 6

Printed on Regency Silk FSC paper
by Cambrian Printers, Aberystwyth, Wales, UK

CONTENTS

INTRODUCTION

There is nothing like eating your own home-grown produce fresh from the garden or allotment, but when the weather has been kind and you end up with rows of runner beans, tiers of tomatoes or a sea of spinach, it can be overwhelming. And what if you have a few fruit trees? In a good year you could be faced with literally hundreds of apples, plums or pears.

If you don't have a garden or allotment, there are still opportunities for excess. For those of you who take the trouble to drive out to your local pick-your-own farm or garden centre, you know it isn't worthwhile just bringing home a couple of small punnets. So it is all too easy to return with the car overloaded and the kitchen soon filled with enormous bowls of strawberries or blackcurrants that need to be dealt with. Even a trip into the countryside can result in several shopping bags full of blackberries if you are lucky enough to find some laden bushes before anyone else gets there.

So the big question is – what can you do with it all?

When you started out sowing your seeds in the spring, or looked forward to the harvest in the summer and autumn, you probably had visions of wonderful culinary delights. Who doesn't love fresh strawberries and cream, apple crumble and custard, carrot and coriander soup or refreshing cucumber salad? But when there is too much of the same produce to cook and eat, you need to think creatively, or the rest of the family will be greeting your next meal with groans and cries of "Not again!" And there is also nothing sadder or more wasteful than a plot of wilting, dried-up yellowing plants or shrivelled pods that you just couldn't face bringing back into the house.

This book is here to help you. Learn how to use your fresh produce in imaginative and unusual ways; how to preserve fruit and vegetables so that you can eat them throughout the year; how to store food so that it doesn't go off; and how to ring the changes on those tired old recipes.

Shopping

Although this book is aimed at helping you find ways to use up fruit and vegetables that you grow or pick yourself, you will also find that, during high season, the same things will be more freely available and much cheaper in your local shops and farmers' markets. So, even if you can't grow some crops in your garden or allotment but still want to take the opportunity to buy any surplus that shops and stallholders are selling cheaply, you will find lots of advice on storing, preserving and cooking them in the pages that follow.

What makes a glut?

Any type of produce grown in too large a quantity can constitute a glut, but there are some vegetables and fruits that regularly cause problems for gardeners. This is either because it is very hard to extend their growing or picking season, or it is too difficult for the average amateur gardener to remember to stagger the planting and sow little and often. After a few months, a whole new crop can suddenly appear and you will need to pick it quickly before it spoils, drops, bolts or runs to seed.

In the UK, the crops most likely to produce a bumper harvest include the following.

Salads – lettuce, radishes and cucumbers.

Vegetables – tomatoes, courgettes and marrows, broad beans, runner beans, green beans, peas, spinach, carrots, beetroot and winter squash.

Soft fruit – blackcurrants and redcurrants, strawberries, blackberries, gooseberries and raspberries.

Other fruit – rhubarb, apples, pears, plums and damsons.

(Although many gardeners also grow large numbers of potatoes, onions and garlic, these crops have not been included here. This is because whole books are devoted to the subject of different ways to cook potatoes, whilst onions and garlic appear as ingredients in nearly all of the savoury recipes provided in this book.)

A successful crop can sometimes seem like too much of a good thing.

So, if you do have a glut of fruit or vegetables, you have a number of choices:

- Eat them straight away – either raw as side dishes, salads or desserts, or cooked to your liking. Look through the book to find a range of ideas for using fresh produce in new and different ways.
- Store them – whole or treated for the freezer.
- Preserve them – by drying them or by adding liquids such as vinegar or alcohol, which will keep your fruit or vegetables recognisable. You could also turn them into chutneys, jams or other long-life products that can happily sit in your store cupboard until you are ready to use them.
- Disguise them – as unusual ingredients that add flavour and moisture to, for example, cakes, breads or fruity savoury dishes.
- Drink them – by turning them into straightforward juices and smoothies or something a little more alcoholic.

Tips and tricks for reducing your glut

To avoid having a serious problem now or in the future, here are a few ways to reduce the size of a glut:

- Pick your produce early. You will get through far more plants this way and so leave fewer crops in the ground or on the trees to increase in size and abundance. Good examples of vegetables that are at their best, or sweetest, when young and tender include runner beans, carrots, courgettes (including the flowers), peas and baby beets. You can also pull up early spring onions to use like chives, and cut lettuce and spinach leaves regularly rather than waiting for the whole head to form. It is also better to use under-ripe fruit for most jams and chutneys.
- Before next year's growing season starts, make an extra effort to check on plant harvesting times. If you replace some of your usual seed packs with varieties that can be picked earlier or later than normal, or that can happily overwinter, you will extend the growing and picking season dramatically and will find your produce much easier to deal with.
- Sow half the usual number of seeds or sets and shake your trees vigorously to remove overcrowded fruit as it develops. This practice should lead to better-quality fruit and vegetables and thus more of the eventual crop being used.
- Grow more plants in containers. If you have beans, spinach, tomatoes, pick-again lettuce, other salads and herbs and even strawberry pots near the back door, you will find that you use them far more than if you have to go down to the bottom of the garden each time you want to prepare a meal.

Raw vegetables and fruit

The simplest way to deal with a glut is to eat whatever you pick straight out of the garden without any cooking at all – simply peeled, grated or sliced.

Runner beans are at their best when young.

Raw or cooked vegetables?

Until recently, we were told that raw food was best and so we happily munched our carrot sticks and drank our tomato juice safe in the knowledge that we were doing ourselves the most good. But recent research has shown that although over-cooking vegetables can certainly result in a loss of vital minerals, enzymes and vitamins, in some instances it is only through cooking that you can produce different nutrients or preserve more of the goodness. This is particularly true for tomatoes, which release lycopene, an antioxidant, when they are cooked. Foods containing antioxidants are an important ingredient in our diets because they are believed to help protect us from free radicals – molecules that can cause damage to cells.

In the same way, breaking up fibrous vegetables such as carrots through cooking and puréeing releases more antioxidants, and is therefore more beneficial than using all your energy to chew the same amount of vegetable raw. So the healthiest option is to eat a mix of raw and cooked fruit and vegetables as, that way, you should get a plentiful supply of all the nutrients they contain.

Fresh fruit

If you need some extra ideas for using your fresh fruit other than just eating it as it comes, chopping it up to make a fruit salad or combining with cream, why not eat it:

- mixed into muesli, cereal or porridge
- as a layer inside a trifle
- between spoonfuls of different-flavoured ice cream or jelly
- blended or stirred into yoghurt
- as a topping or filling for cakes such as cheesecake and Victoria sponge

- as an accompaniment to cheese – apples (particularly good with Cheddar or Wensleydale) and pears (which go well with Stilton or Roquefort) are the most common fruits used in this way, but strawberries complement cream cheeses; plums work with blue cheeses; and redcurrants add contrast to brie or Camembert. (A favourite dessert in our house is digestive biscuits or oatcakes topped with curd cheese and sliced strawberries.)

Fruity salads

As an alternative, you can always add fruit, particularly apples, pears or strawberries, to many salads.

- Slice strawberries and add to an avocado, red pepper and lettuce salad, dressing it with lemon and olive oil.

- Alternate strawberries with thinly sliced cucumber, and dress with white wine vinaigrette (see page 62).
- Mix pear with walnuts, goat's cheese and lettuce and drizzle with a dressing of balsamic vinegar, olive oil and lemon juice.
- Use pear in a sweet and sour salad combined with radishes and cucumber, to which you add curry powder, coriander leaves and a balsamic vinegar dressing.
- Put a spin on the traditional coleslaw recipe by adding some shredded apple into the mix.
- Make an Italian salad from sliced, peeled pears, rocket and shavings of Parmesan (or Pecorino) cheese.
- Combine pears, avocado, red or yellow peppers and lettuce and then toss in a dressing made from vinaigrette blended with blue cheese.

A trip to the local pick-your-own farm often results in a hoard of fruit to deal with.

Chapter 1
Storage methods

Without any treatment at all, there are two ways in which you can store many vegetables and fruits:

- in the ground, leaving them where they are growing
- harvested and stored in a cool, dark room.

For most people, however, the storage method that is most familiar is freezing. To ensure that the produce keeps in top condition when frozen, it should be prepared properly first. This is discussed in this chapter.

Storage methods that involve processing, namely preserving, bottling and drying, are covered in Chapters 8 to 10.

Outdoor storage

There are a few root vegetables, including carrots and beetroot, that can safely be left in the ground until you want to use them, although digging them up during a hard winter might be difficult. To protect them against frost or to stop them rotting in heavy rain, cover them with materials that will trap air, such as wood chips, straw or horticultural fleece. If possible, leave large winter squash to ripen on the vine for as long as possible, but harvest them before the first frosts.

Podded beans such as broad beans and runner beans can be left on the plant to dry out during a dryish autumn (or just pull up the plants and hang the whole stem inside). You can then harvest and use the dried beans in stews and curries, for example, as well as retaining some to plant next year.

Indoor storage

With the weather as unreliable as it is in the UK, a safer option is to bring your produce indoors. You will find that much of it can be stored without any treatment, and far more conveniently, inside – as long as the conditions are right.

Root vegetables

You can store most root vegetables in a cool, dark place such as a basement or garage as long as they are in a perfect, unblemished condition. The ideal temperature is from 0°C (32°F) to 10°C (50°F).

Carrots and beetroot will store particularly well between layers of damp sand or peat, but for most root vegetables you can also brush off any loose earth and pack them, unwashed, in wire or plastic baskets or between layers of sawdust or crumpled newspaper in crates or boxes. (Take care with wooden containers as they may rot in the damp.)

Note: If you do decide to keep the seeds from old beans to eat in the same way as kidney beans or other pulses, soak them overnight and make sure that you boil them hard for 10 minutes first to remove any toxins.

Winter squash will store for months once their skins have cured.

It is a good idea to check your vegetables regularly for any signs of rot and to move them every few weeks so that one spot doesn't stay in contact with the container all the time. It is usually best to choose the larger specimens for storage. If you can, leave an inch or so of stem on the plant to reduce the risk of infection.

Winter squash

Winter squash need to be cured (i.e. left so that their skins have time to harden) for a few weeks and can then be stored on slatted wooden shelves or in baskets. They like slightly warmer and moister conditions than root vegetables so ideally store them at temperatures of 10-13°C (50-55°F).

Tomatoes

Tomatoes can store well if picked when green; they should still ripen – slowly – if placed in paper bags, or in drawers or shallow trays covered in newspaper, or in a black bin bag, loosely tied. Some people say you should add a banana or apple to the mix but I haven't found that necessary, as long as you check the fruit regularly and always include at least one tomato that has nearly ripened, to give off the required ethylene gas.

Fruit

Apples need more airflow than vegetables, and it is usual to wrap them individually in newspaper before storing them in crates and baskets, so that one rotten one does not lead to a spread of infection. Personally, I find the eating apples we typically grow very difficult to keep for long, but some varieties such as Winston do keep well. Cooking apples are much easier and normally last right through the winter and well into spring. Pears can be stored between layers of shredded newspaper but they tend to be more delicate and bruise more easily than apples. They can be kept in a cool cupboard or room but should be checked more frequently and may not last that long. For this reason, it may be best not to treat them like apples and wrap them in newspaper as you won't be able to spot problems until it is too late.

Freezing

The most important thing about freezing is not to freeze anything you wouldn't want to eat as it already is. So, for example, if your runner beans are stringy or your carrots are woody and shrivelled, they will not be improved by sitting in the freezer for a few months.

Almost all vegetables and fruits can be frozen in some form or other, but if they contain a great deal of water, such as courgettes and cucumbers, you will

> **Note:** Any cooked food must be allowed to cool first before it is frozen. Otherwise it will raise the temperature of the freezer and may start thawing frozen food in neighbouring containers.

unfreeze a mushy pulp if you simply put them in bags and then into the freezer. Depending on what you want to do with your produce, you therefore need to choose an appropriate freezing method. It is also a good idea to freeze in portion sizes, so you don't need to defrost your entire stock when cooking for just one or two helpings.

Labelling everything is important; one bag of frozen purée can look very much like another. As well as knowing what is in the bag or box, you should also make a note on the label of when it was frozen, so that you use up food in good time rather than keeping it so long it starts to deteriorate.

One problem with freezing is that it can result in an unpleasant taste and an appearance known as 'freezer burn'. This happens when the pack loses moisture and then dries out and the food reacts with the air. It can be avoided by removing as much air as possible during packing, sealing the freezer packs very carefully, and not keeping the food stored for too long.

Open freezing

For fruit or vegetables to keep their shape when thawing out, it is best to start the process off by spacing them out on trays that you then freeze for about an hour or so. To make them easier to remove once frozen, the trays can be lightly oiled.

Once the individual pieces are solid, pack them together in bags or boxes and they will retain their shape when you use them later. Obviously, if you know you will only want to use the food in a purée or stew, this extra stage is not necessary and you can pack them in bags straight away.

Open freezing is certainly the perfect method for freezing small berries, such as blackberries and raspberries, where you may want to use the fruit as a garnish for your puddings; otherwise, they will unfreeze in a broken and pippy mess.

Fruits and vegetable fruits such as tomatoes should be washed and picked over before being open frozen whole, quartered or chopped. (Although tomatoes will never be anything but mushy when thawed, so don't expect to serve them in salads.) If the fruits have stones, it is better to stone them before freezing so they can be used in cooking straight from the freezer without further

> **Note:** Two different ways to remove air before freezing are:
> - Slowly squeeze the air out of a plastic bag or non-rigid container by pressing around the food without squashing it too much and then sealing firmly.
> - Tie the bag shut around a straw, suck air out of the bag, and then remove the straw quickly and tie the bag tightly.

treatment; it is also possible that the stones might taint the flavour over time.

Blanching

Most vegetables, including sliced runner beans, marrow, winter squash, green beans, carrots, spinach and broad beans,

Peas are best blanched before freezing.

should be blanched before freezing. This process sets the colour and destroys enzymes that cause a loss of flavour, vitamins and texture, and which can limit the time that the vegetables can be kept.

Blanching involves adding the vegetables to boiling water, bringing it back to the boil and boiling for a short time – from a few seconds to a couple of minutes, depending on size and water content – before plunging them into cold water to stop the cooking process. Drain and pat dry before freezing. To avoid over-blanching, it is best to blanch small vegetables such as peas, as well as spinach and tomatoes, for about 1 minute; sliced vegetables or green varieties including broad and green beans for 2 to 3 minutes; and whole root vegetables, such as small carrots, for a few minutes longer.

Although rhubarb can be frozen without any cooking, it improves the flavour and appearance if it is blanched first. Blanch-ing is also a good method to use if you want to peel tomatoes, damsons or plums before freezing as the skins will slip off easily.

When freezing courgettes, you can keep small specimens whole or slice larger ones and either blanch them quickly (no more than about 10 seconds) or fry them in butter or oil for a few minutes instead. Beetroot should be cooked completely rather than blanched, with the tops left on, so that they don't bleed and lose their colour. After cooking, peel them before freezing either halved, sliced or, if very small, left whole.

Sugar packing

Some fruits will keep better and have a better flavour if frozen with sugar. For gooseberries, strawberries, raspberries, redcurrants and blackcurrants that you are going to use for jams or sweet puddings, hull, peel or top and tail, sprinkle with sugar and turn them so they are thoroughly coated. This will draw out some of the juice and keep the fruit firmer. They can then be packed into containers.

For any fruits such as rhubarb that are not so juicy, or for fruit that has been stoned – for example, plums and damsons – layer the fruit in rigid containers covered with a syrup made using 225g (8oz) of sugar dissolved in each 570ml (20fl oz / 1 pint) of water.

Apples are very versatile as you can peel, slice and blanch them and then freeze them unsweetened, coat them in sugar

Note: To keep plastic bags of liquids more stackable, start the freezing process by placing the bag being filled inside a rigid container such as a cardboard box. As soon as the contents have started to solidify, the cardboard can be removed and the bag will continue to hold its square shape.

Stoned fruit is best stored in sugar syrup.

Strawberries can juiced before freezing.

or cover them with sugar syrup. Pears are different as they ripen so fast that it is hard to judge the very best moment to freeze them, so it is probably best to poach them in sugar syrup first before freezing.

Processing

To save space when freezing crops you know you will want to use in drinks, sauces or stews, or if freezing particularly ripe fruit or vegetables, it may be better to process the food first. Extract the juice or prepare a simple purée by liquidising

them with or without sugar. You can also create and freeze a finished sauce, but don't add the final seasoning or spices at this stage.

When ready, pour the juice, purée or sauce into freezer tubs, ice trays (to create frozen ice cubes of purée), boxes or plastic bags.

When filling bags and boxes, it is important to leave room for expansion as the liquid contents freeze, or you may split the container.

Chapter 2
Your produce

MAKING THE BEST USE OF YOUR PRODUCE

There are certain crops that gardeners in the UK seem to grow in abundance, and so the recipes and processing advice in this book aim to cover all of these. If you have too many broad beans or pears, for example, refer to the section in this chapter on that vegetable or fruit for ideas on ways to use them in the kitchen.

There are also many dishes throughout the book that can be made just as well with a 'mix'. For example, vegetable soups, salads, omelettes, stews, pies, pickles and wines can all be made with a wide variety of vegetables. And fruit crumbles, sponges, jams or juices will be equally tasty made from a mix of berries, currants or orchard fruits. So if you have too much of one particular crop, there is no need to limit yourself to the produce listed for each recipe. Instead, use up your glut by using a mix of ingredients.

Equally, if you want to use up a particular fruit or vegetable, you should find that substituting your produce for a similar one named in a recipe will be easy and successful.

Vegetables and salads

This section includes numerous ideas for using up a glut of vegetable and salad crops, including some unusual suggestions.

Beetroot

The tops of young beetroot can be used in a similar way to spinach or chard, although in the UK we mainly cook the roots. As they are rather messy and tend to bleed heavily staining purple juice everywhere, some people prefer to leave peeling them until after they are cooked. You should also try to keep some of the stalk on when cooking them whole, so twist these off when harvesting rather than cutting them off completely.

Beetroot are very quick to cook in a microwave, so you shouldn't think of them as only being ready after hours of long, slow boiling, and although often overlooked as a raw ingredient, they are excellent as a very attractive alternative or addition to cabbage or carrot in salads. They also produce a healthy and colourful vegetable juice and combine well with horseradish sauce, if you enjoy a slightly hotter dish.

Like carrots, courgettes and winter squash, the sweetness of beetroot means that these vegetables can be included in cake recipes as well as savoury dishes. They are also far too nice to be swamped in sharp vinegar.

Specific recipes include:
- Baked vegetable crisps
- Beetroot and apple chutney

Beetroot is surprisingly versatile in the kitchen.

- Beetroot and bean salad
- Beetroot and carrot juice
- Beetroot and cheese topping
- Beetroot and chocolate cake
- Beetroot and horseradish
- Beetroot pâté
- Beetroot purée
- Beetroot relish
- Borscht (beetroot soup)
- Corned beef and beetroot hash
- Hot beetroot and cream
- Pickled beetroot
- 'Pink mash' (see Mash)
- 'Red slaw' (see Coleslaw)

You can also use beetroot for terrines and savoury muffins; have it marinated à la Grecque, fried in rösti, roasted or dried, in bubble and squeak; in pies, tarts, curries, potato bake, casseroles, risotto, pilaf, pancakes, omelettes, frittata or fritters; or use it to make wine.

Broad beans

Sadly, many people do not like broad beans, but that is often because they have only eaten them when they are well past their best and have acquired a rather unpleasant grey-green tinge and bitter aftertaste. Young broad beans can make a wonderful ingredient in many dishes, and if you go to the Middle East you will find that they are a staple vegetable on most menus – usually in the form of fried vegetable cakes, purées or as the main vegetable constituent of meat stews. (In countries such as Egypt they are known as fava beans.)

Young broad beans, or larger beans after skinning, make an attractive salad addition and they can also be included in a surprising number of other dishes.

Specific recipes include:
- Broad bean and bulgur wheat
- Broad bean and pea soup
- Broad bean falafel
- Broad bean purée
- Deep vegetable pie
- Pasta with broad beans
- Potato bake
- Spicy broad bean pâté
- Stir fries
- Vegetable curry
- Vegetable gratin
- Vegetable risotto
- Vegetable sauce for pasta

Carrots straight from the garden.

You can also use broad beans for terrines and savoury muffins; or have them in salads, rösti, bubble and squeak, fritters, pancakes, omelettes, vegetable burgers, casseroles or piccalilli, or marinated.

Carrots
You need the right soil to grow large carrots, but they are a very British vegetable and are always welcome as one of our main root crops. They store well so are available all year round and they can be eaten raw or cooked.

We are all used to serving carrots in soups, grated in salads, added to meat stews or as a vegetable side dish, but they are an extremely versatile vegetable and, like beetroot or winter squash, can also be used in cakes, breads and even ice cream. They form a good base for many pickles and relishes, and are a healthy alternative to potatoes when mashed or sliced for crisps. They can even be used as a meat substitute – for example, in shepherd's pie or bolognese sauce – if you mix them with filling ingredients such as lentils and/or mushrooms. You can also drink them as a juice.

Specific recipes include:
- Baked vegetable crisps
- Beef, tomatoes and green/runner beans
- Beetroot and carrot juice
- Bolognese
- Bubble and squeak

- Carrot and apple salad
- Carrot and celeriac salad
- Carrot and cheese muffins
- Carrot and coriander soup
- Carrot and courgette terrine
- Carrot and fruit juice
- Carrot and pea fritters
- Carrot and raisin loaf
- Carrot cake
- Carrot ice cream
- Carrot salsa
- Carrot, orange and radish salad
- Cheese pastry flan
- Coleslaw
- Corned beef and beetroot hash
- Crudités
- Deep vegetable pie
- Indian carrot pudding
- Mixed vegetable burgers
- Potato bake
- Quick flan or quiche
- Roast carrots

- Roasted carrot pâté
- Rösti
- Shepherd's pie with carrots
- Stir fries
- Sugared carrots
- Tortilla (Spanish omelette)
- Vegetable gratin
- Vegetable samosas
- Vegetables à la Grecque

You can also use carrots for curries, risotto, pilaf, pancakes, frittata or casseroles.

Courgettes and marrows

Marrows are simply overgrown courgettes: they have a tougher skin, can be watery and need more time to cook. It doesn't take long for a small courgette to grow into a huge marrow if the weather is right, and so, unless you are aiming for large specimen plants, you need to

Many gardeners will have experienced a courgette glut.

watch very carefully and pick them as soon as they are a usable size. In some gardening books you will see them labelled as 'summer squash', to distinguish them from other plants in the same family known as 'winter squashes' (e.g. butternut and acorn squash).

There are a number of different varieties of courgette, and they can appear yellow, a very dark green or bright green, and can be more or less striped, so a courgette mix should make an attractive salad or lightly cooked vegetable side dish. Their only real drawback is that, because they contain so much water, cooking them from frozen is not usually that successful unless you are using them in a purée or soup.

Although courgette flowers are often quoted in cookbooks as a recipe ingredient, I have not been attracted to them myself. But there is still very little waste when you use the vegetables in your cooking and, as they are surprisingly versatile, they are possibly one of the best choices if you want to grow a limited range of crops.

Specific recipes include:
- Baked courgettes
- Bottled courgettes
- Bubble and squeak
- Carrot and courgette terrine
- Courgette and chocolate cake
- Courgette and pine nut salad
- Courgette and tomato salsa
- Courgette bread
- Courgette cake
- Courgette chutney
- Courgette omelette
- Courgette purée
- Courgette tea bread
- Courgette wine
- Courgette, basil and tomato salad
- Deep vegetable pie
- Fritters
- Hot piccalilli
- Marrow and ginger jam
- Minestrone soup
- Mixed vegetable burgers
- Potato bake
- Ratatouille
- Roast ratatouille
- Rösti
- Stir fries
- Stuffed vegetables
- Vegetable gratin
- Vegetable sauce for pasta
- Vegetable soup

You can also use courgettes for savoury muffins, roasted vegetable soup, samosas, tarts, curries, risotto, pilaf, stuffed pancakes, tortilla, frittata, pizza, casseroles or soufflés; marinated or pickled; or you could serve them with a cheese sauce.

Cucumbers

Many people do not have a greenhouse and so can only grow the outdoor or ridge cucumber. Fortunately, they have a wonderful flavour, although the thicker, prickly skin and large seeds mean you may prefer to peel and de-seed them before serving.

Cucumbers have always been a very British salad vegetable – and are known throughout the world as a sandwich filling – but they can be made into a vast number of dishes, ranging from delicate cold soups to unusual baked side dishes. They can also be used as an accompaniment to fish or chicken, in dips and relishes, pickled, as a juice, and even in savoury water ices.

Specific recipes include:
- Baked cucumber
- Blended cucumber soup
- Bulgur wheat and cucumber salad (tabbouleh)
- Chicken and cucumber
- Crudités
- Cucumber and lemon juice
- Cucumber and pepper relish
- Cucumber and tarragon sauce
- Cucumber and tomato soup
- Cucumber and yoghurt dip
- Cucumber salsa
- Gazpacho sorbet
- Gazpacho soup
- Greek salad

- Green bean Salade Niçoise
- Green juice
- Pickled cucumbers
- Pear, radish and cucumber sweet and sour salad (see Fruity salads, page 11)
- Salmon, cucumber and strawberries
- Strawberry and cucumber salad (see Fruity salads, page 11)
- Tomato and cucumber relish

Green beans

Variously grown as dwarf, string, French or climbing beans, these are a classic vegetable to serve with most meat and fish dishes. Yet they can also make excellent warm salads and can be added to many soups, stews or pickles when you want a little crunch or extra flavour. As one of three types of bean described in this book (the others being broad and runner), green beans are the least likely to fill me with dread when a large bag of

Pick French beans regularly for a continuous crop.

them arrives from the garden. This is partly because they are not quite so awful as the other types of bean when they are a little on the mature side, but also because it is quite surprising how many lightly cooked green beans one family can happily eat at a single sitting.

As well as in recipes that include green beans specifically, you can use green beans in any runner bean dish.

Specific recipes include:
- Beef, tomatoes and green/runner beans
- Beetroot and bean salad
- Deep vegetable pie
- Green bean pâté
- Green bean Salade Niçoise
- Green beans and garlic (see Runner/ green beans and garlic)

- Stir fries
- Tortilla (Spanish omelette)
- Vegetable risotto
- Vegetable sauce for pasta
- Warm green bean salad

You can also use green beans for soups, crudités, rösti, bubble and squeak, fritters, curries, pilaf, pancakes, gratin, casseroles, chutneys, pickles and wine, or marinate them.

Lettuce

As you will know from the supermarket shelves, the range of colours, leaf shapes and varieties of lettuce is astounding. As well as using fully hearted plants, you can eat lettuce leaves as you go, tearing them gently off the outside of the growing plant, which happily carries on putting out new leaves for months.

Lettuce comes in a variety of wonderful leaf shapes and colours.

Grown together with other leafy vegetables such as spinach, mustard, corn salad (lamb's lettuce) and rocket, it means that you will have interesting salads every time you go out and pick a quick handful of leaves. This is a wonderful way to have cheap mixed salads that are typically so expensive in the supermarkets.

Lettuce is hardly ever cooked, which is a pity as it can form an interesting alternative to cabbage or spinach in many dishes. If you've never cooked it before, as well as using it in the recipes below, why not try substituting it for spinach in some of the spinach recipes (see page 31)?

Specific recipes include:
- Braised lettuce and peas
- Caesar salad
- Green bean Salade Niçoise
- Lettuce soufflé
- Lettuce soup
- Stir fries
- Waldorf salad

You can also use lettuce in sandwiches and salads, to accompany any cold savoury dish, or with burgers. Its leaves make ideal 'cups' for holding meatballs, spicy salads or flavoured sliced or minced meat, such as chicken or beef. You can include lettuce in risotto or even add sliced lettuce to fried or stewed dishes just like any other vegetable, although you should add it near the end and only cook it until it is just wilting but still green.

Marrows
See Courgettes and marrows, page 25.

Peas
The latest fad is pea tendrils in salad, but for most of us the pea is one of the most familiar vegetables from our childhood (particularly served with mashed potato) and one of the few that fussy eaters tend to be able to face. Personally, I love eating raw peas, but they are not to everyone's taste, and so you may prefer only to serve them cooked.

If you like pods, then mangetout or sugar peas are worth growing alongside ordinary peas, and all can be used in a very wide range of recipes. They seem to go with most things, including eggs, rice and pasta, and so for any recipe requiring a mix of vegetables, always include some peas for a deeper flavour, colour and/or texture.

Specific recipes include:
- Braised lettuce and peas
- Broad bean and pea soup
- Carrot and pea fritters
- Curry
- Deep vegetable pie
- Mixed vegetable burgers
- Pea purée
- Shepherd's pie with carrots
- Tortilla (Spanish omelette)
- Vegetable risotto
- Vegetable samosas
- Vegetable soup

You can also use peas in terrines, savoury muffins, minestrone, salads, rösti, bubble and squeak, tarts, flans, pasta dishes, pilaf, pancakes, omelettes, frittata, gratin, potato bake, stir fries or casseroles, or for making wine.

Perpetual beet

See Spinach, opposite.

Radishes

Although there are large radish varieties that you can cultivate, you are most likely to have a glut of the quick-to-grow, smaller varieties – such as Red Globe or French Breakfast – which are often sown as a 'filler' vegetable between rows of slower-growing plants. We usually forget to use the leaves, but they are equally edible and can be treated like a peppery version of spinach.

Radishes are related to horseradish and can be quite hot when raw, although they are easily tamed by cooking. Their main culinary use is sliced in salads or whole in crudités, and it is worth popping into the garden whenever you are going to make a salad or sandwich so you can add a cut-up radish and help use up a large crop.

Perhaps we need to rethink the radish and eat it more as people in the Far East eat their mooli or daikon radishes: fried or stewed lightly with salt and soy sauce, or mixed with cabbage, cucumber or spinach. In Japan and Korea radishes are treated as a crunchy alternative to above-ground vegetables, but they can also be seen as one of our more unusual root vegetables as they can be roasted or baked as well. Although at their best eaten raw, this versatility means that it is well worth trying to use them more often. This will help the humble radish become a more accepted addition to British meals.

Specific recipes include:

- Baked vegetable crisps
- Carrot, orange and radish salad
- Crudités
- Pear, radish and cucumber sweet and sour salad (see 'Fruity salads', page 11)
- Radish relish
- Roasted radishes
- Sautéed radishes

You can also use radishes in soup, rösti, fritters, risotto, stir fries, salsas or pickles, or marinate them.

Runner beans

Nothing uses up the vertical space in a garden so well as runner beans, and they can also look very attractive with their white or scarlet blossoms.

Runner beans are not very edible once they start maturing, and it is definitely not a good idea to pick and freeze old beans as they will taste even worse when you come to cook them. Instead, pick them early and eat them as small and fresh as possible. For me, that means before they reach the stage where you have to string them, so I prefer to fill the freezer with very young beans rather than harvest them late in the summer.

As well as a side dish, runner beans are excellent added to pies and curries with other vegetables, and you will also find recipes in this book for unusual ways to serve them, including in soups, pasta sauce, chutneys or pickles. Many of the recipes in this book refer to green beans, so if you have a glut and want to substitute runner beans, it should make little difference.

Specific recipes include:
- Beef, tomatoes and green/runner beans
- Runner bean chutney
- Runner bean soup
- Runner bean wine
- Runner beans and garlic (see Runner/green beans and garlic)
- Vegetable curry
- Vegetable gratin
- Vegetable sauce for pasta

You can also use runner beans for pâté, savoury muffins, salads, crudités, rösti, bubble and squeak, pastry, risotto, pilaf, omelettes, frittata, stir fries, casseroles or piccalilli, or have them marinated or pickled.

Spinach

It can be quite hard to grow spinach without it bolting early in the season, but if you find perpetual beet or Swiss chard easier, you can treat them in a similar way and substitute them in many of the recipes. (Personally, though, I would only use these two vegetables raw in salads as baby leaves, and you will find that, as well as having a slightly stronger taste than spinach, they can be less moist, the stalks can be tough and they can take longer to cook.)

Spinach is particularly versatile as a raw salad crop and I always add it with lettuce and other leaves to my salads. It is packed full of iron and vitamins and gives a lovely colour to any dish.

It is also very easily frozen and can be used in a wide variety of dishes, such as soups, soufflés, pasta, pies, curries, as a

Spinach makes an excellent salad leaf.

pizza topping or pancake filling, baked with eggs (Florentine style), or even in 'green' drinks.

Specific recipes include:
- Apple and green leaf juice
- Chicken and spinach yoghurt curry
- Green juice
- Hot bacon salad dressing
- Sautéed spinach
- Spinach and eggs Florentine style
- Spinach börek
- Spinach lasagne
- Spinach pakora
- Spinach pesto
- Spinach soufflé (see Lettuce/spinach soufflé)
- Stuffed pancakes
- Vegetable soup

You can also use spinach in minestrone soup, pasticcio, risotto, pilaf, rösti, fritters, omelettes, frittata or gratin; in filled pasta or in any green leaf salad.

Squash (winter)

The two most common types of winter squash grown in the UK are butternut and acorn, but most of the varieties have a creamy or yellow flesh and a nutty flavour, and, although a speciality vegetable a few years ago, they have now become part of our staple diet.

Squash bake, roast and mash very easily to make a perfect alternative to potatoes, and the flesh can also be used in a wide variety of ways, including in cakes, soups and gratins. Their shape also means they work well as a stuffed vegetable.

Specific recipes include:
- Butternut squash cupcakes
- Roast winter squash
- Roasted winter squash soup
- Squash and coconut pudding
- Squash butter
- Squash pâté
- Stuffed vegetables
- Vegetable risotto
- Vegetable soup
- Winter squash pie
- Winter squash tea bread

You can also use squash with pastry; in savoury muffins, minestrone, rösti, bubble and squeak, fritters, baked vegetable crisps, pasta sauce, curries, gratin, soufflé or casseroles; mashed or baked; or even in ice cream.

Swiss chard

See Spinach, page 31.

Tomatoes

Few vegetables are as versatile as the tomato, and – although they do need some sun – in a good summer they will grow prolifically outdoors.

Although technically a fruit, tomatoes are rarely served as a dessert, but that is probably the only area of this book where you will not find relevant recipes. They can be turned into soups, sauces and drinks; they are the automatic choice for many pasta or pizza dishes; and they are even useful for savoury jam (marmalade) or, when under-ripe, in that old favourite, green tomato chutney.

Specific recipes include:
- Aubergine and tomato bake
- Baked fish, pesto and tomatoes
- Beef, tomatoes and green/runner beans
- Bolognese
- Bottled tomatoes (passata)
- Courgette and tomato salsa
- Courgette, basil and tomato salad
- Cream of tomato soup
- Cucumber and tomato soup
- Dried tomatoes
- Gazpacho sorbet
- Gazpacho soup
- Green tomato chutney
- Italian beef with dried plums
- Pissaladière
- Pizza
- Potato and tomato salad
- Ratatouille
- Roasted tomato purée
- Stuffed vegetables
- Tomato and basil salsa
- Tomato and bread soup
- Tomato and cheese tart
- Tomato and cucumber relish
- Tomato and sultana chutney
- Tomato flatbread

Green tomatoes soon ripen, or can be used in chutney.

- Tomato ketchup
- Tomato marmalade
- Tomato purée
- Tomato salad
- Tomato sauce
- Tomato sorbet

Fruit

Listed in this section are many recipes for the overabundance of fruit you may be growing or picking this year.

Apples

There is very little that needs to be said about apples, as we love them and use them in so many ways that they are probably the British favourite fruit. This is supported by the fact that we celebrate Apple Day every year on 21 October. As well being delicious in fruit puddings and cakes, apples can form an unusual but valuable addition to savoury dishes such as curries, salads, chutneys and roast meats (as apple sauce) as well as helping with the setting of jams and jellies. When you have a glut and the lawn is covered with windfall fruit, there are two excellent ways to deal with large numbers (after chopping out all the bad bits): freeze bags of purée or turn them into bottles of cider.

Specific recipes include:
- Apple and blackberry cordial
- Apple and green leaf juice
- Apple and plum butter
- Apple and raisin tea bread
- Apple bread
- Apple fritters
- Apple jelly
- Apple purée
- Apple relish
- Apple snow
- Apple, peach and pear juice
- Baked apples
- Beetroot and apple chutney

Celebrate Apple Day in October.

- Blackberry (and apple) jam
- Braised apple and red cabbage
- Candied fruit
- Carrot and apple salad
- Carrot and fruit juice
- Cheesecake with apple
- Chinese toffee apples
- Cider
- Cooked fruit leathers
- Coleslaw
- Cooking apple chutney
- Courgette chutney
- Cranberry, apple and pear sauce
- Damson tansy
- Danish fruit dessert
- Dorset apple cake
- Dried apple rings
- Dried fruit compote
- Eve's pudding (see Fruit sponge)
- Fruit crumble
- Fruit pancakes
- Green juice
- Green tomato chutney
- Low-calorie blackcurrant smoothie
- Marrow and ginger jam
- Mincemeat
- Plum and apple chutney
- Plum, apple and strawberry juice
- Pork à la Normande
- Spiced pear chutney
- Spotted Dick
- Summer (or autumn) pudding
- Toffee apple upside-down cake
- Toffee apples
- Waldorf salad

You can also use apples to make apple pies, Tarte Tatin, apple ice cream or sorbet; and can add them to wine to make mixed fruit wine or to curry for an 'English' variant.

Blackberries

In southern England, blackberries are ripe in mid-August, but further north you will have to wait until September to pick your fruit. To make sure that you don't include any ants or woodlice, steep blackberries in salt water for a few minutes before rinsing thoroughly. You will be able to pick out all the little insects that emerge before you start cooking!

Because of their seeds, blackberries are not as popular as other berries, but they combine well with any variety of berry or currant as well as apples, pears or plums, and they can be a perfectly acceptable substitute in almost any recipe for raspberries, blackcurrants or redcurrants. You can also sieve any purée for more palatable jellies or smoothies.

Specific recipes include:
- Apple and blackberry cordial
- Blackberry (and apple) jam
- Blackberry cakes
- Blackberry coulis (see Blackcurrant/ blackberry coulis)
- Blackberry vinegar
- Pear and blackberry flan
- Pickled blackberries
- Raspberry and blackberry soup
- Summer (or autumn) pudding

You can also use blackberries for pies, crumbles, sponges, cheesecakes, fools, pancake fillings, smoothies, liqueurs and fruit wine, and with other fruits for ice cream or sorbets.

Blackcurrants

A favourite currant, blackcurrants will dominate any dish, and so when mixing them with other fruit, such as strawberries, plums or raspberries, take care not to use too many or they will swamp the flavour completely. Having said that, blackcurrants are absolutely delicious and make the very best jam, as well as some of the most fantastic ice creams, crumbles and pies. They are stronger and woodier than redcurrants, and, when I was growing up, my favourite pudding was my mother's redcurrant and blackcurrant pie, which to my mind is the perfect combination.

Blackcurrants are a bit of a nuisance to prepare, as you have to remove stalks and leaves quite carefully and, unlike redcurrants, they don't come off the stems very easily (or hang in such convenient bunches for picking!), but they freeze very well and cook down to a good strong purée for desserts or drinks. Make the cordial in this book, for example, and you will never need to buy a bottle of Ribena again.

Specific recipes include:
- Blackcurrant cordial
- Blackcurrant coulis (see Blackcurrant/ blackberry coulis)
- Blackcurrant jam
- Blackcurrant juice
- Blackcurrant liqueur
- Easy fruit ice cream
- Fruit crumble
- Fruit water ice (sorbet)
- Low-calorie blackcurrant smoothie
- Mixed fruit muffins
- Redcurrant and blackcurrant pie
- Summer berry preserve
- Summer (or autumn) pudding

Sun-ripened blackcurrants.

If your damsons are particularly sour you will need to add an extra ounce or two of sugar to the quantities specified.

Specific recipes include:
- Damson cheese
- Damson and gin liqueur
- Damson tansy
- Easy fruit ice cream
- Fruit crumble
- Marrow and ginger jam
- Tarte Tatin

You can use damsons to make brandy, or simply have them as dried fruit.

You can also use blackcurrants for sponges, fools, cheesecakes, fruit vinegar or wine, or in smoothies.

Gooseberries

Damsons

If you haven't eaten them before, you may think that damsons would be horribly sour, but in fact the ripe fruit is juicy and sweet and very similar to plums, although the flesh is more greengage than plum and there is definitely a tangy undertone that may not appeal to everyone. We have about ten damson trees in our small garden, as it was originally part of an orchard, but if you don't grow your own you can still find wild damsons on country walks or on laden trees leaning over kitchen walls as, strangely, many people simply don't bother to pick the fruit at all.

You can use damsons as a substitute for plums in many of the pudding or preserve recipes, including damson ketchup (see Tomato ketchup, page 186).

Gooseberries are related to blackcurrants and redcurrants and they are very easy to grow without the need for much interference from the gardener. Early varieties are not often eaten raw as they are too tart (until they suddenly seem to over-ripen and go mushy and yellow). Although you can grow late-fruiting dessert varieties that are sweet enough to eat raw, they are not so good for cooking. Gooseberries have a high pectin content, making them ideal for jams and jellies, for example, but you will definitely want the sharp green varieties for this.

Gooseberries make delicious puddings when stewed and sweetened (but, as they lose most of their green colour when cooked, they unfortunately tend to make desserts look a little uninterest-ing). They are also similar to apples in that they can be happily married with meat or fish – classically with mackerel, but gooseberry sauce goes extremely well with any fatty or smoked meat, such as duck or pork.

Gooseberries are commonly combined with elderflowers, so if you grow any or can find them in your area, infuse the hot liquid for your gooseberry recipe with the flowers for a few minutes before straining and using.

Specific recipes include:
- Gooseberry and raspberry smoothie
- Gooseberry cake
- Gooseberry fool
- Gooseberry jam
- Gooseberry sauce
- Gooseberry soup

You can also use gooseberries for sponges, crumbles, summer pudding, poached fruit, stuffed pancakes, ice cream, sorbet and pies, as well as juices, cordials and wine.

Pears

I love pears and have tried using them in many dishes in place of apples. Although this can work very well, and it is certainly worth experimenting with some of the recipes in this book, pears do have a much lighter flavour than apples, and when I tried substituting them in apple purée to serve with roast pork, and in apple cake and sponge pudding, the pears on their own turned out to be far less successful and also more watery in texture. My advice would therefore be to use a mixture of apples and pears if you want to use up your pears like this.

On the other hand, pears make a wonderful and unusual ingredient in salads and are hard to beat as a dessert when poached gently with sugar and spices. They go particularly well with vanilla, almond and chocolate, and make very juicy drinks and lovely ice creams and sorbets. They are also, to my mind, far more successful dried than any other fruit I have tried.

Specific recipes include:
- Apple, peach and pear juice
- Baked pears and plums
- Bottled pears
- Candied fruit
- Cranberry, apple and pear sauce
- Easy fruit ice cream
- Fruit pancakes
- Pear and blackberry flan
- Pear, radish and cucumber sweet and sour salad (see Fruity salads, page 11)
- Pear salsa
- Pear tea bread
- Pear upside-down cake
- Pear, chocolate and nut pudding
- Pear, rocket and Parmesan salad (see Fruity salads, page 11)
- Pear, walnut and goat's cheese salad (see Fruity salads, page 11)
- Pears, pork and blue cheese
- Poached pears
- Poires belle Hélène
- Spiced pear chutney
- Spiced pickled pears
- Spotted Dick

You can also use pears to make perry, and they are nice simply as dried fruit.

Plums

There are so many varieties of plum and also a range of sizes, from tiny cherry or Mirabelle to the larger Victoria or red plums. All can be cooked in the same way but the small ones, once stoned, will cook down and will not look so attractive in preserved or bottled fruit recipes where large halves are the norm.

Like apples, you can use plums in many savoury settings; plum sauces, pickles or chutneys go well with meat or cheese and, famously, are the most well-known fruity accompaniment to Chinese aromatic duck pancakes. Plums are also a good choice as the base for many alcoholic drinks.

Plums are a particularly good alternative to apples and so make a perfectly accept-able substitute in most apple pudding recipes if you want to use up a glut.

Specific recipes include:
- Apple and plum butter
- Candied fruit
- Cooked fruit leathers
- Dried fruit compote
- Easy fruit ice cream
- Fruit crumble
- Italian beef with dried plums
- Jamaican pancakes
- Marrow and ginger jam
- Mixed fruit wine
- Pickled plums
- Plum and apple chutney
- Plum and onion relish
- Plum and orange sorbet
- Plum cake
- Plum clafoutis
- Plum jam
- Plum liqueur
- Plum sauce
- Plum Tarte Tatin
- Plum, apple and strawberry juice

- Plums in brandy
- Summer (or autumn) pudding

You can also use plums in sponges, bread pudding, tea bread, Danish fruit dessert, upside-down cake, mixed fruit muffins; in jelly or ketchup; with almonds in a tart, or dried in fruit cake. They can also be poached or baked, or are nice simply dried.

Raspberries

In our family, this is the soft fruit par excellence. You will have noticed that in the shops raspberries always cost twice as much as strawberries or blackcurrants, even though they aren't particularly hard to grow, so having a glut of this majestic fruit is not often seen as a disadvantage.

Raspberries freeze quite well, although, like other soft fruit, they don't last more than a few days in the fridge. Fortu-nately, they can also be turned into purées as well as being easily mixed with sugar, alcohol or vinegar for jams or a range of drinks. Raspberries, like redcurrants, have also become acceptable as an accompaniment to certain savoury dishes, and this makes them even more flexible than some other soft fruit.

Specific recipes include:
- Easy fruit ice cream
- Eton mess
- Gooseberry and raspberry smoothie
- Jamaican pancakes
- Mixed fruit muffins
- Raspberry and orange smoothie
- Raspberry and nut tray bake
- Raspberry and redcurrant cordial

- Raspberry coulis (see Raspberry/strawberry coulis)
- Raspberry jam
- Raspberry salsa
- Raspberry soup
- Raspberry vinegar
- Summer berry preserve
- Summer (or autumn) pudding

You can also combine raspberries with any mixed fruit, so you can always use them up in crumbles, sponges, fools, sorbets or wine.

Redcurrants

To me, redcurrants have a cleaner taste than blackcurrants, although the two types of currant work really well together in desserts such as pies, crumbles and sponges, and you can easily substitute redcurrants for blackcurrants in a wide range of desserts. They grow in a similar way, but redcurrants are easier to harvest as their bunches hang down more freely and they are easy to strip off the twigs – just run a fork down the stem.

As blackcurrants and blackberries turn purple in cooking, use redcurrants with strawberries, raspberries or more exotic fruit such as mangoes or pineapples if you want a 'red' dessert. They also make lovely red jellies, purées and sauces, and a beautiful pink ice cream – for example, when mixed with apple.

Specific recipes include:
- Fruit sponge
- Raspberry and redcurrant cordial
- Redcurrant and blackcurrant pie
- Redcurrant cheese
- Redcurrant jelly
- Summer berry preserve
- Summer (or autumn) pudding

Redcurrants are so easy to grow in the British climate.

You can also use redcurrants with any berry mixture for juice, wine, crumbles, pastries, pancakes, ice cream, sorbets, vinegars or cakes.

Rhubarb

There are various different types of rhubarb grown in the UK, ranging from giant reds to those with pale green stems, but perhaps the most well known is Champagne rhubarb. Young, pink rhubarb stems are a delicacy and are quite pricey in the shops, so being able to pick your own is very satisfying. There is usually room in even the smallest garden for a single plant that will grow whatever the weather or type of soil. However, two or even three plants can produce quite a large number of stems and so, with rhubarb being to some extent an 'acquired taste', finding the right recipe and using the best-quality fruit can be very important. When creating desserts containing rhubarb, it is wise to use the youngest, freshest sticks possible. Otherwise, your finished dish may develop a rather thick and gluey texture and take on an unpleasant greeny-brown colour.

Once their thickened bases and poisonous leaves have been removed, sticks of rhubarb will keep very well for a few days in the fridge. Unlike cooking apples, rhubarb requires lots of sugar in order to be palatable, but since Victorian times it has been used for many of the same 'nursery' puddings as apples or gooseberries, including those firm favourites –crumble, pie, fool and sponge. Sweetened purée is particularly good in fruit pancakes, Danish fruit dessert, ice cream, sorbet or summer (or autumn) pudding.

If you want to spice up your rhubarb, the two flavours that go particularly well with it are ginger and almond.

Specific recipes include:
- Fools
- Fruit crumble
- Fruit sponge
- Mixed fruit wine
- Rhubarb and almond tart
- Rhubarb and strawberry cordial
- Rhubarb and strawberry smoothie
- Rhubarb relish

You could also use rhubarb instead of marrow, in rhubarb and ginger jam.

Strawberries

The strawberry season is a long one, but strawberries are one of the few soft fruits that do not freeze well whole or keep for any length of time in the fridge. Once you have used them fresh in your desserts, you may need to employ a number of different processing methods in order to continue serving your strawberry glut throughout the year.

Strawberries do make exceptionally good jam, of course, but they are also easy to freeze in the form of a purée, which can then form the basis for a wide range of dishes, such as coulis, soups, smoothies, ice creams or cordials.

Specific recipes include:
- Easy fruit ice cream
- Eton mess
- Plum, apple and strawberry juice

Strawberries need eating or processing quickly, as they don't last that long.

- Rhubarb and strawberry cordial
- Rhubarb and strawberry smoothie
- Salmon, cucumber and strawberries
- Strawberry, avodado and red pepper salad (see Fruity salads, page 11)
- Strawberry and banana smoothie
- Strawberry and cheese spread
- Strawberry and cucumber salad (see Fruity salads, page 11)
- Strawberry coulis (see Raspberry/strawberry coulis)

- Strawberry flan
- Strawberry fool
- Strawberry jam
- Strawberry soup

You can also add strawberries to many family puddings, such as crumbles, sponges, summer pudding, pancakes or sorbets, or use them in fruit wine. Or you can even dip them in chocolate for a real treat.

In the following chapters, where possible, the number of servings that a recipe will make has been indicated, but of course this will vary with individual appetites! Serving amounts have not been included for most side dishes, sauces, preserves and drinks, as in these cases they are much more difficult to define.

Chapter 3
Starters and salads

PÂTÉS AND TERRINES

Pâtés are minced or blended meat, fish or vegetables that are either
eaten as a spreadable paste or formed into a 'cake' that is baked in
the oven and then cut into slices. They can be served either hot or
chilled with toast or flatbreads such as pitta. About 450g (1lb) of
vegetables will make enough pâté to serve 4 as a starter.

Terrines are also baked mixtures, but the vegetables are often prepared
separately so that you get an attractive layered effect.

Green bean pâté

450g (1lb) green beans, trimmed

1 onion, chopped

Olive oil

85g (3oz) walnut pieces

1 tbsp wine vinegar

To season: Salt and pepper

1 Cook the beans in a little water for about 6-10
minutes.

2 Gently fry the onion in the oil until soft and
transparent.

3 Mix all the ingredients and blend to a pâté-like
consistency. If necessary, add a little extra
cooking water or oil.

4 Season to taste.

Spicy broad bean pâté

450g (1lb) broad beans, podded

1 garlic clove, chopped

2-3 tbsp olive oil

1-2 tbsp lemon juice

1/2 tsp cumin, ground

1 tsp paprika, ground

To season: Salt and pepper

Optional: 85g (3oz) Parmesan
cheese, grated

1 Cook the broad beans for 3-6 minutes, then
cool and skin.

2 Blend lightly with the garlic, oil, lemon juice and
spices; it is nicer if left fairly rough.

3 Season well and, if necessary, add a little extra
oil and some lemon juice if the mixture is too
thick.

For a more solid mixture, stir in the cheese.

✻ You could serve the blended spicy broad bean pâté sprinkled with
extra paprika, or, for a more solid pâté, spoon the mixture into a greased
baking tin, cover with foil and bake for 30-40 minutes in a medium oven.

Roasted carrot pâté

340g (12oz) carrots, chopped

2 cloves garlic, quartered

2 tbsp tahini paste

1/2 tsp cumin, ground

1 tbsp olive oil

To season: Salt and pepper to taste

You will also need: Blender

1   Wrap the carrots and garlic in foil and roast at 180°C (360°F / Gas Mark 4) for about 1 hour. Cool.

2   Add to the rest of the ingredients and liquidise in a blender.

3   If necessary, add a little extra oil and season to taste.

Carrot and courgette terrine

For a special effect, as well as using puréed vegetables you could add a layer of lightly blanched whole vegetables, such as peas or broad beans, between two of the layers.

Serves 4

225g (8oz) carrots, steamed/cooked in a microwave

225g (8oz) courgettes

225g (8oz) mushrooms

40g (1 1/2 oz) butter

3 eggs, beaten

6 tbsp single cream

2 tbsp parsley, chopped

2 tbsp thyme, chopped

2 tbsp chives, chopped

To season: Salt and pepper

For the sauce:

2-5 tbsp puréed cooked green vegetables, e.g. peas or beans

200ml (7fl oz) white sauce / single cream

Salt and pepper

You will also need: Blender

1   Lightly fry the courgettes and mushrooms separately in the butter.

2   Purée the three different vegetables separately, then combine each mixture with 1 beaten egg and 2 tbsp cream. Mix the chives with the carrots, the parsley with the courgettes, and the thyme with the mushrooms.

3   Season the vegetable mixtures well.

4   Grease a 1lb (45g) loaf tin and spoon the mushroom mixture into the bottom to make an even layer. To make it easier to turn out the terrine, you could first line the tin with greased baking parchment.

5   Spoon the carrot mixture on top of this layer and finally spoon in the courgette mixture. (Or make more, thinner, layers by using half the mixture and repeating the layers for each purée.) Level the top.

6   Cover with foil or waxed paper and stand the loaf tin in a separate tin half-filled with hot water.

7   Bake the terrine at 200°C (400°F / Gas Mark 6) for about 1 hour until the centre when tested with a knife is completely firm.

8   Cool for 15 minutes, then turn out on to a plate.

9   Serve in slices with a sauce made by combining green vegetable purée with cream or a white sauce and seasoning well.

Beetroot pâté has an amazing colour, but don't be put off!

Beetroot pâté

450g (1lb) beetroot

2 onions, chopped

1 garlic clove, chopped

Olive oil

1 tsp cumin, ground

1 tbsp lemon juice

To season: Salt and pepper

To garnish:
Coriander, fresh, chopped

1 Wash the beetroot well and boil or microwave until tender. When cool, peel and chop roughly.

2 Fry the onions and garlic in oil for a few minutes until transparent.

3 Blend the beetroot, cumin, lemon juice and onion mixtures together until smooth. Add extra oil or lemon juice if it is too thick.

4 Season well.

5 Cool and serve garnished with chopped coriander.

Squash pâté

450g (1lb) squash, halved/ quartered, seeds removed

4 tbsp lemon juice

1/2 tsp coriander, ground

1 garlic clove, chopped

4 tbsp olive oil

To season: Salt and pepper

To garnish:
Coriander, fresh, chopped

You will also need: Blender

1 Bake the squash for 30-40 minutes in a roasting tin at 180°C (360°F / Gas Mark 4) or steam the squash and then scrape the flesh off the skin.

2 Blend with the other ingredients and season to taste.

3 Serve scattered with coriander.

BREAD TOPPINGS

As well as starters like pâté, served with bread, you can use vegetables to make a bread topping where the bread is an integral part of the dish. Any type of bread you have to hand will do, but French and Italian breads seem to work particularly well. (The tomato bruschetta recipe also works well with tomato flatbread; see page 175.)

Tomato bruschetta

Serves 2

1 French stick / 1 baguette / sliced ciabatta

4-6 tomatoes, ripe

1 garlic clove, crushed

1-2 tbsp olive oil

2-3 tsp balsamic vinegar

4-6 basil leaves, fresh, chopped

Salt and pepper

Optional: Red onion, chopped; Cheese, e.g. goat's or mozzarella

To serve: Olive oil, tomatoes

1. Toast the bread or drizzle with oil and bake in the oven until golden brown.

2. Peel (if preferred) and chop up the tomatoes.

3. Mix in a bowl with the garlic, olive oil, vinegar, basil, salt and pepper. Alternatively, rub the garlic over the bread just before serving, rather than mixing it in with the tomatoes.

4. If you like onion, mix some red onion in with the tomatoes.

5. To serve, drizzle some extra oil over the toast and then cover with spoonfuls of the tomato mixture.

✱ For a more substantial dish, cover the bread with slices of cheese, such as mozzarella or goat's cheese, before topping with the tomato mixture.

Beetroot and cheese topping

Ciabatta / wholemeal bread, sliced

Beetroot, cooked

Goat's cheese – 30-55g (1-2oz) per person, sliced

Balsamic vinegar

Chives, chopped

Several walnuts, crushed

Olive oil

To season: Salt and pepper

To serve: Lettuce

1   Grill the cheese on a foil-covered baking dish for a few minutes until just melting.

2   Cover the sliced bread with slices of beetroot and then drizzle over some vinegar.

3   Top with the grilled goat's cheese then scatter with chives and walnut pieces.

4   Drizzle on a little olive oil.

5   Season well and serve with lettuce leaves.

SAVOURY MUFFINS

Although muffins are normally thought of as small sweet cakes, you can create savoury versions by combining vegetables such as beans, spinach, beetroot or carrots with cheese, herbs, spices, porridge oats or nuts to make an unusual snack or light lunch.

To use different vegetables, simply substitute the same amount of grated or chopped vegetable(s) for the carrots in the recipe below. You could also include different cheeses and/or nuts; for example, try spinach with ricotta and walnuts, beetroot with feta cheese, or courgettes with Cheddar, basil and pine nuts.

* To make your own buttermilk (as in, for example, the carrot and cheese muffin recipe overleaf), add a few tablespoons of lemon juice to ordinary milk and leave for 5-10 minutes.

Carrot and cheese muffins

Makes 12 muffins

285g (10oz) plain flour

1 tbsp baking powder

1/2 tsp bicarbonate of soda

170g (6oz) carrot, grated

85g (3oz) Cheddar/Parmesan cheese, grated

2 eggs

55ml (2fl oz) vegetable oil

200-255ml (7-9fl oz) buttermilk / milk / soured cream / yoghurt

Salt and pepper

Optional:
Extra cheese

30g (1oz) red onion, chopped

Substitute 85g (3oz) of the flour for porridge oats

You will also need:
12 paper cases / individual muffin tins

1   Sift together the flour/oats, bicarbonate and baking powder.

2   Stir in the carrot, onion (if using) and cheese.

3   Beat the eggs and oil together and stir in to the mixture.

4   Start adding the buttermilk/milk/cream/yoghurt until you have a soft dropping consistency.

5   Season well.

6   Fill 12 paper cases or individual muffin tins and bake at 200°C (400°F / Gas Mark 6) for 15-20 minutes. Test that the muffins are done by inserting a knife blade; it should come out clean.

7   For a cheesier version, you could sprinkle extra cheese over the tops of the muffins before putting them in the oven.

Savoury muffins make an excellent addition to a lunchbox.

SOUPS

Soup is an extremely good way to deal with a glut, as you can make a soup base with almost any vegetable and it will freeze very well. You can then use your personal choice of herbs or spices to create something special.

Soups are also very versatile: they can range from a delicate dinner-party starter to a hearty lunch; you can eat them at work or on a day out, either hot or chilled, if you store them in a thermos flask; and they can aid your weight-loss diet, as the same food is absorbed more slowly in liquid than solid form.

As a general rule, 570ml (20fl oz / 1 pint) of stock (or other liquid) usually makes enough soup for two good portions; scale up all the ingredients if you are cooking for more people. The quantities of vegetables you use are also very flexible – but if in doubt add a little extra, or the soup may end up rather thin-tasting.

Cream of tomato soup

4 large tomatoes, chopped

1 medium onion, chopped

1 celery stalk, chopped

1 garlic clove

2$^{1}/_{2}$ tbsp butter

1 tbsp flour

285ml (10fl oz / 1/2 pint) chicken or vegetable stock

140ml (5fl oz / 1/4 pint) cream

1/2 tsp salt

A few basil leaves, torn

1/2 tsp parsley, chopped

You will also need: Blender

1   Melt the butter and gently fry the garlic, celery and onion.

2   Add the tomatoes and the salt and cook for 5 minutes.

3   Stir in the flour and then add the stock.

4   Simmer for a further 10 minutes.

5   Liquidise the soup and then return to the pan.

6   Add the cream and herbs and cook on a very low heat for a further 10 minutes to develop the flavours.

Lettuce soup

2-3 heads lettuce, chopped

1 small onion, diced

55g (2oz) butter

30g (1oz) flour

285ml (10fl oz / 1/2 pint) chicken/vegetable stock

Parsley and mint, chopped

285ml (10fl oz / 1/2 pint) milk

To season: Salt and pepper

To serve: Parmesan cheese, grated

You will also need: Blender

1 Melt the butter and soften the lettuce and onion for 5 minutes.

2 Stir in the flour and then add the stock.

3 Season and add the herbs.

4 Bring to the boil and simmer for 10-15 minutes.

5 Liquidise, return to the pan, add the milk and heat through.

6 You may like to serve the soup scattered with grated Parmesan.

Tomato and bread soup

Serves 3-4

1 onion, chopped

1 garlic clove, chopped

85ml (3fl oz) olive oil

680g (1lb 8oz) tomatoes, chopped

2 tbsp basil, chopped

2-3 slices bread, without crusts, broken into pieces

Optional: Tomato purée

To season: Salt and pepper

1 Fry the onion in the oil for a few minutes, add the garlic and continue cooking gently for a few more minutes.

2 Add the tomatoes and simmer for 5 minutes.

3 Add half the basil, the bread pieces and the tomato purée (if using), as well as enough water to keep the mixture sloppy.

4 Simmer for about 15 minutes.

5 Season well and serve garnished with the rest of the basil.

Which oil?

Either olive or vegetable oil can be used for frying, but vegetable oil is best when cooking at high temperatures or where you don't want the stronger flavour of olive oil to be obvious in the finished dish.

Vegetable soup

225-340g (8-12oz) vegetables,
e.g. peas, courgettes, beans,
carrots or spinach, well
washed, peeled and chopped

1 onion, chopped

1-2 tbsp oil / 30g (1oz) butter

Handful of herbs, e.g. parsley,
tarragon or basil, chopped

570ml (20fl oz / 1 pint) chicken
stock / vegetable stock (or half
stock, half milk)

To season: Salt and pepper

Optional:

1 medium potato, diced

1 garlic clove, crushed

To serve: Yoghurt/cream

You will also need: Blender

1   Gently fry the onion in oil until transparent. Add
    the garlic, if using, and fry for another minute or
    so.

2   Add the vegetables and cook for a further 5
    minutes to soften. Include potato if you like a
    thicker soup.

3   Add the herbs and stock (or milk/stock mixture)
    and bring to the boil. Now turn down the heat
    and add any milk.

4   Simmer for 10-15 minutes until tender.

5   Season well.

6   Liquidise and, for a very smooth soup, strain
    through a sieve.

7   Serve as it comes, or stir in a spoonful of yoghurt
    or cream.

For variety:

* Add chopped or
crushed chillies for
a hot soup.

* Spice up spinach
soup with nutmeg.

* Add chopped
mint to pea soup.

Carrot and coriander soup

1/2 tbsp oil

1 medium onion, sliced

340g (12oz) carrots, diced

1 tsp coriander, ground

570ml (20fl oz / 1 pint) stock

To season: Salt and pepper

To garnish: Coriander leaves, fresh, chopped

You will also need: Blender

1. Heat the oil and gently cook the onion and carrots for 1-2 minutes to soften.
2. Stir in the ground coriander and cook for 1 minute.
3. Add the stock, bring to the boil and simmer for 20-30 minutes until the vegetables are tender.
4. Liquidise, season and serve garnished with coriander.

Borscht (beetroot soup)

1 large beetroot / several small beetroots, well washed

1 carrot, chopped

1 potato, peeled and chopped

1 onion, chopped

1 garlic clove, chopped

Oil or butter

1 tbsp lemon juice / wine vinegar

570ml (20fl oz / 1 pint) stock

To season: Salt and pepper

To serve: Sour cream / yoghurt; Chives, chopped

You will also need: Blender

1. Cook the beetroot for a few minutes in a microwave or simmer in stock until tender. Check by poking it with a knife.
2. Cool, then peel and chop, retaining any cooking liquid.
3. Fry the onion gently in the oil or butter for about 10 minutes, adding the garlic after 5 minutes.
4. Add the cooked beetroot, other vegetables, stock, cooking liquid, lemon juice / vinegar and seasoning, and cook for about 10-15 minutes until the vegetables are all soft.
5. Cool and then liquidise in a blender.
6. Reheat to serve and garnish with swirls of sour cream or yoghurt and a scattering of chives.

Minestrone soup

This hearty soup combines vegetables with (often) fried bacon, pulses such as cannellini beans, and small pasta shapes or broken spaghetti. Apart from the vegetables mentioned in the recipe, you can add any others you have available, including celery, green beans, potatoes, cabbage or leeks.

As this soup is not blended, chop the vegetables into bite-sized pieces.

1 tin (300g/10 1/2 oz) pulses, e.g. cannellini beans

2-3 bacon rashers, chopped

2-3 carrots, chopped

1 red onion, chopped

1 garlic clove, chopped

2 courgettes, sliced

4 large tomatoes, chopped

30-55g (1-2oz) spinach

Olive oil

1 small glass red wine

570ml (20fl oz / 1 pint) stock

Herbs, e.g. basil, chopped

2 bay leaves

55g-85g (2-3oz) pasta

To season: Salt and pepper

To serve: Bread; Parmesan cheese, grated

1. Gently fry the bacon with the onion, garlic and carrots for 10 minutes.

2. Add the rest of the vegetables together with the herbs and continue cooking for 5 minutes.

3. Stir in a small glass of red wine, the stock and the beans.

4. Season well and simmer gently for 20 minutes.

5. Now add the pasta and continue simmering until the pasta is cooked and the flavour of the soup has developed.

6. Serve with bread and grated Parmesan.

Runner bean soup

510g (1lb 2oz) runner beans, sliced

1 large onion, chopped

1 large carrot, chopped

2 tbsp butter

710ml (25fl oz) vegetable stock

To season: Salt and pepper

You will also need: Blender

1. Heat the butter in a large saucepan and gently fry the onion for 5-10 minutes until soft.
2. Add the beans, carrot and stock, bring to the boil and then simmer, covered, for about 20 minutes, until the vegetables are soft.
3. Liquidise in a blender.
4. Season well.

Roasted vegetable soups

Although it takes longer, you may like to try roasting some of the vegetables you are going to use for your soups first. If you do this you should find that your soup is sweeter and the flavour more intense – usually particularly true for tomatoes, onions, peppers, carrots, beetroot, courgettes and winter squash.

Roasted winter squash soup

1 medium squash, halved, de-seeded, chopped

2-3 red peppers, de-seeded, chopped

1 red onion, chopped

Olive oil

570ml (20fl oz / 1 pint) vegetable stock

Optional: 1/2 tsp chilli paste

To season: Salt and pepper

1. If you want a hotter soup, dot the vegetables with a small amount of chilli paste before roasting.
2. Turn the vegetables in oil and then roast in a baking tin at 200°C (400°F / Gas Mark 6) for about 40 minutes.
3. When all the vegetables are soft, add them to the stock and blend well. (You don't have to peel the squash but if you use old, hardened specimens you may prefer to scrape off the flesh before adding to the stock.)
4. Check the seasoning before serving.

Chilled soups

On a hot day, there is nothing quite as refreshing as a cold summer soup, which you can make with either fruit or vegetables.

Broad bean and pea soup

450g (1lb) broad beans, podded (if old, blanch and remove skins)

225g (8oz) peas

1/2 onion, chopped

30g (1oz) butter

570ml (20fl oz / 1 pint) vegetable stock

2-3 sprigs mint

4-6 tbsp plain yoghurt

To season: Salt and pepper

Optional: 1/4 tsp curry paste

You will also need: Blender

1. Fry the onion gently in the butter for a few minutes.
2. Add the stock and bring to the boil.
3. Add the broad beans, peas and mint, and simmer for 15 minutes.
4. Remove the mint and purée the soup in a blender.
5. Stir in the yoghurt. (If you want a curry flavour, stir the curry paste into the yoghurt before adding it to the soup mix.)
6. Blend again for 1 minute.
7. Chill for several hours and check seasoning before serving.

Cucumber and tomato soup

1 large cucumber, diced

1 tsp salt

285ml (10fl oz / 1/2 pint) plain yoghurt

285ml (10fl oz / 1/2 pint) single cream

285ml (10fl oz / 1/2 pint) tomato juice

1 garlic clove, finely chopped

570ml (20fl oz / 1 pint) stock

Handful fresh mint, chopped

To season: Salt and pepper

To garnish: Mint/chives, chopped

1. Sprinkle salt over the cucumber and leave to drain for 30 minutes to draw out the liquid.
2. Rinse thoroughly and dry well on kitchen paper.
3. Mix together all the other ingredients and then stir in the cucumber.
4. Season well and then chill.
5. To serve, garnish with further mint or chives.

Blended cucumber soup

1 tsp butter, unsalted

3 large cucumbers, peeled, cut into pieces

570ml (20fl oz / 1 pint) vegetable stock / chicken stock

115ml (4fl oz) white wine

1 tbsp fresh dill

Pinch of nutmeg, ground

140ml (5fl oz / 1/4 pint) sour cream

115ml (4fl oz) plain yoghurt

To season: Salt and pepper

To garnish: Sour cream; Cucumber, sliced

1 Melt the butter, add the cucumber and soften gently for about 10 minutes.

2 Add the stock, bring to the boil and then add the white wine.

3 Reduce the heat and simmer for about 10 minutes, stirring frequently.

4 Add most of the dill and a pinch of nutmeg and season to taste.

5 Blend until smooth and allow to cool.

6 Add the yoghurt and most of the sour cream and whisk until smooth.

7 Chill for several hours.

8 Serve garnished with a spoonful of sour cream, cucumber slices and dill.

Gazpacho soup

Serves 3-4

1 red pepper

1 green pepper

1/2 onion

1 cucumber, peeled

1 garlic clove, crushed

6 ripe tomatoes

1-2 slices bread, stale, without crusts

2 tbsp olive oil

3 tbsp red wine vinegar

Handful of parsley / coriander leaves

Optional: Tomato juice

To season: Salt and pepper

To garnish: Red pepper, diced; Cucumber, diced; Croutons (squares of bread fried in olive oil)

You will also need: Blender

1 Blend all the ingredients and add tomato juice or water if the mixture is too thick.

2 Season to taste and chill for at least an hour before serving.

3 For a smoother soup, de-seed the tomatoes before blending, or sieve the vegetable purée before blending in the bread.

4 Either sprinkle the garnish on the soup before serving, or provide the garnish ingredients in separate bowls.

Fruit soups

Strangely, it is possible to use fruit in soups, although the result will clearly not be the same as a normal vegetable soup. Try serving them on hot summer evenings as an unusual dinner party course or as a light dessert.

Raspberry and blackberry soup

Serves 1-2

115g (4oz) raspberries

115g (4oz) blackberries

285ml (10fl oz / 1/2 pint) buttermilk (or milk left for 10 minutes after adding a few drops of lemon juice)

285ml (10fl oz / 1/2 pint) yoghurt

1 Sieve the raspberries and stir in half the buttermilk and half the yoghurt. Set aside in a dish.

2 Repeat with the blackberries in a separate dish.

3 Chill both dishes.

4 When ready to serve, spoon the raspberry mixture into serving bowls and top or marble with the blackberry mixture.

Fruit soup makes an unusual but delicious starter.

Gooseberry soup

500ml (18fl oz) water

450g (1lb) gooseberries,
topped and tailed

1/2 stick cinnamon / lemon zest

3 tbsp sugar

Pinch of salt

3 tbsp cornflour

To serve:
Soured cream / whipped cream

1 Cook the gooseberries, spices, salt and sugar gently with the water for about 10-15 minutes.

2 Make a paste of the cornflour with a little water and add to the stewed fruit.

3 Cook for a few more minutes until the mixture thickens.

4 Check the taste and, if necessary, add more sugar.

5 Chill and serve garnished with soured or whipped cream.

Strawberry soup

Serves 1-2

225g (8oz) strawberries, puréed

225ml (8fl oz) dry white wine

55g (2oz) sugar

225ml (8fl oz) orange juice

1 Boil the wine and sugar for 5 minutes.

2 Leave to cool and then stir in the strawberry purée and orange juice.

3 Chill for several hours.

Raspberry soup

Serves 1-2

2 tbsp honey

5 tbsp red wine

225ml (8fl oz) water

450g (1lb) raspberries, sieved

140ml (5fl oz / 1/4 pint) soured cream

1 Dissolve 2 tbsp honey in 2 tbsp red wine and 2 tbsp water heated gently.

2 Cool and stir in the raspberries, soured cream and remaining water.

3 Mix thoroughly and serve well chilled.

SALADS

When you plan to make a salad, remember that almost any leaves or even stems can be used to add flavour and variety. So you could include, for example, fresh spinach leaves, radish tops, beetroot tops, pea shoots, rocket, mustard, lettuce or lamb's lettuce. Try also to make use of any fresh herbs you can find.

As well as ingredients that you would expect to find in a salad, such as radishes, lettuce, cucumber and tomatoes, you can also add raw vegetables that are normally eaten cooked. These include fresh peas, broccoli and cauliflower florets, or finely diced, sliced or grated sprouts, celeriac, courgettes, carrots and beetroot. And don't forget blanched, skinned broad beans or sliced green or runner beans.

For extra protein, stir through cubed cheese, smoked fish or cold meat, and add more crunch with a sprinkle of toasted nuts and/or seeds, such as pumpkin or sunflower. If you want a more substantial dish, you can include cooked pasta or rice, and/or could incorporate bread – either toast it or fry cubes to make croutons, or simply tear up pitta or other breads and add to the salad ingredients.

Where quantities are unspecified, the salads will serve 2-3 people.

Pear and rocket salad is a popular first course in Italy.

Dressings

The most common oil to use in salad dressings is olive oil, but you can substitute nut oils such as sesame, hazelnut or walnut if you prefer. There is also a huge choice of other dressing ingredients, including lemon juice, wine vinegar and fruit- or herb-flavoured vinegars as well as the darker balsamic vinegar. For an added kick, stir in mustard or chopped hot peppers.

If you like a thicker, creamier dressing, substitute peanut butter, yoghurt, crème fraiche, soured cream or mayonnaise for the oil – or add this as well.

Garlic nearly always improves a salad and can be wiped around the bowl, crushed and stirred into the dressing or chopped up with the ingredients.

Vinaigrette salad dressing

The following quantities are very much a matter of taste, as some people like a more oily dressing.

3 tbsp olive oil

1 tbsp lemon juice / wine vinegar

To season: Salt and pepper

Optional: Mustard

1 Mix the lemon juice, wine vinegar, seasoning and mustard (if using) in a bowl and then slowly whisk in the oil.
2 Once half has been added, taste and continue adding oil until it is right for you.

Everyday salads

There are thousands of salads – summer and winter – that you can make. Here are just a few of the more well-known ones, as well as some unusual salads to try.

Beetroot and bean salad

For a colourful salad, combine cooked purple beetroot with lightly cooked green beans, white cheese such as goat's or feta, and brown walnuts.

Carrot and apple salad

Toss grated carrot and red-skinned apples in lemon juice and honey. If you like, add raisins. Season well and sprinkle with toasted almonds or sesame seeds.

Greek salad

Typically this contains chopped tomatoes, red onion, cucumber and red or green peppers. Add cubed feta cheese and black olives and garnish with fresh or dried oregano. Drizzle over lemon juice or white wine vinaigrette dressing.

Tomato salad

Sliced tomatoes go particularly well with garlic, shredded basil leaves and vinaigrette. For a more substantial dish, add slices of mozzarella cheese. This then becomes the classic Italian Insalata Caprese that is commonly served at the start of an Italian meal.

Coleslaw

As well as the usual mix of grated white cabbage, carrot, onion and sometimes apple in a mayonnaise dressing, you can replace or supplement the white cabbage in coleslaw with grated raw beetroot (with or without grated red cabbage). This salad is often described on menus as 'red slaw'.

A grated cabbage and beetroot salad can also be made with oil and vinegar dressing, if you aren't keen on mayonnaise.

Two famous 'named' salads

Waldorf Mix walnut pieces, chopped apples and celery on a bed of lettuce and dress with mayonnaise and lemon juice.

Caesar Mix crisp lettuce with Parmesan cheese shavings, anchovies (optional) and a strong dressing made from garlic, mustard, Worcester sauce, lemon juice and olive oil. Toasted bread croutons can be added as a garnish.

Crudités

For a change, serve a variety of raw vegetables cut into matchsticks ('julienne' vegetables) or slices or broken into florets, along with a garlicky aioli dip. The best vegetables for this are firm ones such as carrots, cucumber, green beans, celery, radishes, broccoli and cauliflower.

Aioli

Combine ready-made mayonnaise with crushed garlic, a little mustard and lemon juice, and season to taste. Or if you prefer to make your own mayonnaise and can eat raw egg, pound 1 garlic clove, some salt and pepper, and a few tablespoons of lemon juice in a mortar or use a blender. Beat in 2 egg yolks and then slowly whisk in enough olive oil to produce a thick and creamy sauce.

Carrot, orange and radish salad

You may have served chicory (endive) and orange salad, and this is a similar sweet and sour crunchy dish.

2 carrots

6-8 radishes

1 orange, peeled

To dress: Olive oil; Lemon juice

To season: Salt and pepper

1 Peel and coarsely grate the carrots and slice the radishes thinly.

2 Slice the orange and break up the sections into bite-size pieces.

3 Toss all the ingredients with oil and lemon juice and season well.

Carrot and celeriac salad

1/2 medium celeriac

2-3 carrots

To dress:

2-3 tbsp mayonnaise

1 tbsp lemon juice

Caraway seeds

1 tsp mustard

1 Peel and grate the celeriac and carrots.

2 Mix together the rest of the ingredients to make a dressing and then stir in the grated vegetables.

Green bean Salade Niçoise

This is a salad that can contain almost anything, so add tuna, anchovies, potatoes or eggs if you want a hearty meal or if people like them.

100g (3 1/2 oz) green beans, lightly cooked

1 small lettuce

4-6 ripe tomatoes, quartered

1/2 cucumber, peeled and sliced

55g (2oz) black olives

Optional:
4-6 anchovies

1 red onion, sliced

2 hard-boiled eggs, peeled and sliced

200g (7oz) tinned tuna

100g (3 1/2 oz) new potatoes, cooked

To dress: Vinaigrette with crushed garlic

To garnish: Chopped herbs, e.g. parsley or basil

1 Arrange the lettuce leaves in a bowl.

2 Pile the rest of the ingredients attractively on top.

3 Drizzle over the dressing and garnish with chopped herbs.

Bulgur wheat and cucumber salad (tabbouleh)

115g (4oz) bulgur wheat

1/2 cucumber, chopped

2 spring onions, chopped

Mint, chopped

Parsley, chopped

Optional:
200g (7oz) red kidney beans

To dress:
Olive oil

Lemon juice / white wine vinegar

To season:
Salt and pepper

1 Pour boiling water on to the grains and leave, covered, for 15 minutes. If any liquid is left after this time, drain well and press the grains gently to dry.

2 Mix with the rest of the salad ingredients, adding kidney beans for a more substantial dish, and then dress with lemon juice / vinegar and oil, and season to taste.

Courgettes sliced into ribbons make an unusual and attractive salad ingredient.

Courgette and pine nut salad

For this salad, you will either need tender young courgettes or you can quickly chargrill the courgette strips on a griddle pan before combining them with the rest of the ingredients.

2-3 courgettes

Herbs, e.g. parsley, tarragon or basil

To dress:
Olive oil; Lemon juice

To season:
Salt and pepper

To garnish: Pine nuts

1 Slice the courgettes lengthways into very thin ribbons using a mandolin or potato peeler.

2 Mix in a bowl with the chopped herbs.

3 Dress with oil and lemon juice and season well.

4 Toast a handful of pine nuts without oil in a non-stick pan until just starting to brown and then sprinkle over the salad.

Courgette, basil and tomato salad

2 courgettes

Pesto / basil, chopped

Dried tomatoes

To season:
Salt and pepper

To serve:
Parmesan cheese

1 Use a mandolin or simply cut the courgettes into thin matchsticks ('julienne' vegetables).

2 Mix with a little pesto or chopped basil.

3 Add finely chopped dried tomatoes that have been stored in oil (see page 221).

4 Season well and serve with shavings of Parmesan cheese.

Warm salads

On a cool day, you can combine freshly cooked food, such as boiled eggs, duck, chicken, prawns, bacon or beef, with salad ingredients and eat them whilst they are still hot. For example, grill marinated steak, cut into strips and serve on a bed of leaves and sliced tomatoes, drizzled with your favourite salad dressing.

Hot bacon salad dressing

2-3 bacon rashers

Butter or oil

To dress:
2 spring onions

Black pepper

Wine vinegar

1/2 tsp mustard

1   Diced the bacon and cook in butter or oil until crisp.

2   Make a dressing of finely diced spring onions, pepper, wine vinegar and mustard. You will probably not need any salt.

3   Stir in the bacon.

4   Use to dress a bowl containing lettuce or spinach leaves or lightly cooked vegetables such as courgettes, broad or green beans.

Warm green bean salad

225g (8oz) green beans

To dress:
Vinaigrette dressing;
Garlic

Optional: Tomatoes /
red peppers, chopped

1   Cook the beans for a few minutes. Slightly undercook them so they retain a crunch. Drain well.

2   Toss them in a vinaigrette dressing and add a little crushed garlic. Eat while still warm.

3   For added colour, mix in other salad ingredients such as chopped tomatoes or red peppers just before serving.

Potato and tomato salad

450g (1lb) new potatoes

3 bacon rashers

200g (7oz) cherry or
sliced tomatoes

To dress:
Balsamic vinegar;
Olive oil

To season: Salt and pepper

1   Boil the potatoes.

2   Fry the bacon rashers and then chop them into small pieces.

3   Mix together with the tomatoes.

4   Dress with balsamic vinegar and olive oil.

5   Season well.

Chapter 4
Side dishes

SERVING VEGETABLES

MARINATED VEGETABLES

COOKED SALAD VEGETABLES

FRIED VEGETABLES

Fritters

Indian fried vegetables

ROAST VEGETABLES

VEGETABLE CRISPS

SERVING VEGETABLES

A variety of freshly picked beans, carrots, beetroot or spinach will always add flavour and colour to your meals. You can serve them steamed, lightly boiled or cooked for a few minutes in a microwave, either leaving them plain or tossing them in melted butter before serving. Chopped herbs such as parsley, tarragon, thyme or basil make an attractive garnish for most vegetables and you can also add nutmeg or cinnamon to spinach and carrots.

When coping with a glut, you also need to be able to serve your vegetables differently from time to time, so that family members don't get bored with your usual side dishes. One way to spice up the vegetable part of a meal is to create unusual or colourful combinations. For example, sliced carrots, squash, beetroot, beans or tomatoes can all be cooked in the same way – combine any mix with garlic, onion and herbs and then season well and fry gently until just tender.

The most well-known combination dish of this type is ratatouille. Although traditionally made with aubergines, I usually make the dish without, as I don't often have that particular vegetable available.

Mash

As well as potato, most root vegetables and squash make excellent mash. Simply cook them in a little water until soft (or roast squash in the oven), flavour with chopped herbs, season well and then mash to remove all lumps. You may want to add milk and butter.

For a lovely pink mash, mix half boiled potato with half boiled and peeled beetroot (plus some horseradish if you like it hotter) and finish with butter and milk in the normal way. You could also serve pure beetroot mash.

As an alternative, serve puréed vegetables such as beans and peas instead of mashed potato.

Ratatouille

Serves 2

2-3 courgettes, sliced

1 red pepper, sliced

1 onion, sliced

1 garlic clove, diced

3-4 large tomatoes, chopped

Parsley

Olive oil

To season: Salt and pepper

1. Fry the onion and garlic gently in the oil for a few minutes to soften.
2. Add the courgettes and red pepper and cook for a further 5-10 minutes.
3. Add the tomatoes and parsley and simmer gently for 15-20 minutes, making sure that they don't burn. If necessary, add a little water.
4. Season to taste.

Braised apple and red cabbage

Serves 2

1/2 small red cabbage, sliced

1 cooking apple, peeled and sliced

1 onion, chopped

1 tsp nutmeg

1 tsp cinnamon, ground

2-3 whole cloves

3 tbsp white wine vinegar

2-3 tbsp sugar

Oil

To season: Salt and pepper

1. Fry the onion in the oil for a few minutes and then add the cabbage and apple to the pan. Cook for a further 2-3 minutes.
2. Add the spices, vinegar and sugar and simmer for 5 minutes.
3. Season well and cook over a low heat for 30-40 minutes, adding extra water if necessary.
4. As an alternative, cook this in a covered oven dish or roasting tin in the oven at 170°C (340°F / Gas Mark 3) for about 40 minutes.

Baked courgettes

Several small courgettes

Olive oil

To dress:

Balasmic or red wine vinegar

Herbs, e.g. tarragon or parsley, chopped

Salt and pepper

1. Drizzle the oil over the whole courgettes in a baking dish.
2. Season well.
3. Bake in the oven at 180°C (360°F / Gas Mark 4) for about 15 minutes.
4. Dress with the vinegar, more oil, salt and pepper and a handful of chopped herbs.

Beetroot and horseradish

Serves 2

Several beetroot, cooked,
peeled, sliced

140ml (5fl oz / 1/4 pint) yoghurt

2 tsp creamed horseradish

1/2 tsp Dijon mustard

To season: Salt and pepper

To garnish: Chives, chopped

To serve: Roast meat

1 Mix together the yoghurt, mustard and horseradish and season well.

2 Spoon the sauce over the beetroot.

3 Garnish with chives and serve with roast meat.

Sugared carrots

This is a particularly good way to get rid of a glut of carrots that are getting large and old.

Serves 2

2-3 large carrots, peeled, sliced

Handful of parsley, chopped

30g (1oz) butter

Salt

1 tbsp sugar

1 Place the carrots and parsley in a pan and add just enough boiling water to cover the vegetables.

2 Sprinkle on salt and sugar and add the butter.

3 Bring back to the boil and simmer gently for 10 minutes. Nearly all the water should have evaporated.

It's quite easy to turn old carrots into a delicious vegetable dish.

Hot beetroot and cream

Serves 2

1-2 large beetroot(s), cooked, peeled and sliced

Parmesan cheese, grated

140ml (5fl oz / 1/4 pint) cream

Breadcrumbs made from 1-2 slices bread

Butter

Optional:
1 garlic clove, crushed

To season: Salt and pepper

1. Arrange a layer of beetroot slices in a buttered baking tin, packing them tightly together.
2. Add a little crushed garlic (if using).
3. Scatter over some Parmesan cheese and season well.
4. Repeat the layers until you have used all the beetroot.
5. Pour the cream into the dish, cover the vegetables with a layer of breadcrumbs and dot with butter.
6. Bake for about 20 minutes at 180°C (360°F / Gas Mark 4).

Sautéed spinach

Serves 2

30g (1oz) butter

1 garlic clove, crushed

225g (8oz) young spinach leaves

Salt and pepper

1-2 tbsp lemon juice

1 tsp nutmeg

1. Heat the butter and then stir in the garlic and spinach.
2. Once coated, add the rest of the ingredients and fry gently for a couple of minutes.
3. Turn off the heat but cover the vegetables and leave them in the hot pan. They will be wilted and ready to serve after about 5 minutes.

Runner/green beans and garlic

Serves 4

510g (1lb 2oz) beans, chopped/sliced

2 cloves garlic, finely chopped

2 tbsp olive oil / 30g (1oz) butter

To season:
Salt and pepper

1. Heat the oil/butter in a pan and cook the beans and garlic gently for a few minutes.
2. Add a few tablespoons of water and then simmer for 8-10 minutes, adding more water if the pan starts to dry out.
3. Season well.

MARINATED VEGETABLES

One elegant way to serve cold vegetables is to cook them à la Grecque. This involves poaching vegetables such as young courgettes, broad beans, beetroot or baby carrots in a mixture of wine, oil, vinegar and herbs and then letting them cool before serving sprinkled with freshly chopped herbs. You can use red or white wine and can add extra ingredients such as chopped garlic or tomatoes.

Vegetables à la Grecque

Serves 2

225g (8oz) any prepared vegetables

200ml (7fl oz) dry white wine

115ml (4fl oz) olive oil

115ml (4fl oz) lemon juice / white wine vinegar

1 tsp coriander seeds

1 tsp salt

4 peppercorns

1 bay leaf

1 tsp herbs, e.g. thyme, tarragon or parsley, chopped

100ml (3 1/2 fl oz) water

To season: Salt

To garnish: Parsley/tarragon, chopped

1 Mix all the poaching ingredients in a large pan.

2 Bring to the boil and cook on a high heat for a few minutes.

3 Add the vegetables, adding any root vegetables a few minutes before the rest.

4 Simmer gently for 5-10 minutes until just tender.

5 If you prefer, remove the vegetables with a slotted spoon and continue to cook the liquid for a further 5-10 minutes to reduce it by half.

6 Pour the liquid over the vegetables and leave to cool or chill overnight in the fridge.

7 Remove the peppercorns and bay leaf, add a little extra oil and seasoning if necessary and serve garnished with herbs.

COOKED SALAD VEGETABLES

If you have always thought of lettuce, cucumber and radishes as only fit for a salad, it is refreshing to find that they also make welcome and unusual cooked vegetable dishes. Here are just a few to try.

Baked cucumber

Serves 2

1 cucumber

Butter

Herbs, e.g. dill, basil, chives, tarragon

To season: Salt and pepper

1 Top and tail a washed cucumber and then cut into chunks. For large cucumbers, peel and remove the seeds.
2 Add to a microwave dish with butter and mixed herbs. Season.
3 Microwave for 3-5 minutes, or bake in the oven at 180°C (360°F / Gas Mark 4) for 15-20 minutes.

* To enrich hot vegetables like cucumber, stir in double cream just before serving.

Braised lettuce and peas

Serves 2

1 onion, sliced

1-2 lettuce(s), quartered/ shredded

200ml (7fl oz) stock

225g (8oz) peas

100ml (3 1/2 fl oz) cream

Olive oil / butter

1 Fry the onion gently in the oil or butter until soft but not coloured.
2 Add the lettuce and cook for 3-4 minutes.
3 Add the stock and peas.
4 Cover and cook for a further 2-3 minutes.
5 Add the cream and simmer, uncovered, for another 5 minutes until the lettuce is just tender.
6 If there is too much liquid, reserve the lettuce and boil down the juices for a few minutes before serving.

Radishes are more than just a raw salad ingredient – try cooking them for a change.

Sautéed radishes

Serves 2

10 large radishes with tops still intact

2 cloves garlic, finely chopped

1 tbsp olive oil

1 tsp salt

Optional:

Sesame oil

1   Top and tail the radishes and cut them into large chunks or slice them finely.

2   Wash and chop the leaves, discarding any tough stems.

3   Heat the olive oil and lightly fry the garlic for a few minutes.

4   Stir in the chopped radishes and cook for a further 2-3 minutes before adding the leaves.

5   Add the salt and then cook for a few minutes more until the leaves look like cooked spinach.

6   You may like to sprinkle over a little sesame oil before serving.

Roasted radishes

Serves 2

10-12 radishes, washed, trimmed, sliced vertically

Sesame oil / peanut oil

Sesame seeds

Soy sauce / lemon juice

To season: Salt

1   Coat the radishes with sesame or peanut oil and roast for about 20 minutes, turning at least twice.

2   Scatter on sesame seeds and a good drizzle of lemon juice or soy sauce and continue baking for another 5-10 minutes.

3   Season well with salt.

FRIED VEGETABLES

Shallow-frying in a little butter or olive oil can be a healthy way to cook many grated or sliced vegetables, and it is so quick and tasty. A griddle with raised ridges will give the vegetables a more chargrilled flavour.

Adding toasted almonds or pine nuts before serving can also add a new slant to common vegetables.

Rösti

This is a European dish where grated vegetables are formed into solid 'cakes', which are then gently fried in oil or butter. You can also make smaller rösti by frying spoonfuls of mixture or baking them at 200°C (400°F / Gas Mark 6) for 25 minutes.

Serves 2

2 medium carrots, peeled

Other root vegetables, e.g. beetroot or parsnip, peeled

1 large potato, peeled

1 courgette, grated

1 onion, chopped

Vegetable oil / butter

Optional: Thyme

To season: Salt and pepper

1 Parboil the carrots, potato and any other root vegetables and then drain and grate.

2 Mix the courgette with the onion and other vegetables.

3 Season and add any herbs.

4 Heat the oil or butter in a frying pan and add the vegetable mixture.

5 Press this down and cook for about 5-10 minutes until brown.

6 Turn it over to brown the other side.

Bubble and squeak

This dish is an excellent way to use up left-over cooked vegetables, as long as you include enough mashed potato to hold them together.

Potatoes, mashed

Onion or spring onion, sliced

Mixed vegetables, e.g. beans, carrots, beetroot, courgettes

Oil

To season: Salt and pepper

1 Mix together the mashed potato, chopped cooked vegetables, and the sliced onion or spring onion, making sure that you season well.

2 Form into little cakes and fry gently in the oil to brown both sides.

Fritters

One versatile dish is the vegetable fritter, for which you can use any type of vegetables.

To make fritters, mix chopped, grated or sliced vegetables, either raw or pre-cooked, with egg and flour and perhaps grated cheese. Drop spoonfuls of the mixture into a pan and shallow fry both sides.

Carrot and pea fritters

Serves 2

2 large carrots, grated

55g (2oz) peas, lightly cooked

1 onion, grated

1 egg

2-3 tbsp plain flour

1 tbsp cheese, e.g. Cheddar or Parmesan, grated

Chopped herbs, e.g. parsley or coriander

Oil for frying

To season: Salt and pepper

1   Squeeze out as much water as possible from the carrots and onion and then mix with the other ingredients and season well. Add extra flour if the mixture is still a little wet.

2   Heat the oil and then drop in spoonfuls of mixture.

3   Do not stir, and wait until the base is crispy and brown before turning the fritters over.

Vegetable fritters are a great idea for a tasty light lunch.

Battered vegetable fritters

A different type of fritter can also be created by dipping pieces of vegetable in batter and then deep-frying them. This is suitable for sliced courgettes, cauliflower or broccoli florets, or carrot or beetroot sticks, for example.

Prepared vegetables (sliced, florets, etc.)

Batter:

1 egg, separated

1/4 tsp salt

100g (3 1/2 oz) plain flour

140ml (5fl oz / 1/4 pint) milk

Oil

Optional: A little oil / melted butter

1 Stir the egg yolk into the flour and salt.

2 Slowly add enough milk and any oil/butter, stirring constantly, until the mixture forms a batter with the consistency of double cream.

3 Just before serving, whisk the egg white and stir it in.

4 Dip the vegetables in the batter and fry quickly in deep hot oil. (You could also drop spoonfuls of grated vegetables into the batter mixture and then scoop out spoonfuls to fry.)

5 Make sure the fritters are cooked on both sides and then remove from the oil with a slotted spoon. Drain on kitchen paper.

Indian fried vegetables

Two of the most common Indian vegetable side dishes that we eat in the UK are pakoras and samosas.

Pakoras are a mixture of vegetables and a flour batter made with a special gram flour (from chickpeas) rather than ordinary flour or matzo meal. If you cannot find gram flour, you can substitute self-raising flour.

Samosas are like little vegetable pasties that are deep-fried. You could buy filo or special samosa pastry – and some people even make them with tortillas – but it is quite easy to make your own pastry cases as well as the filling.

Samosas are one of India's most famous vegetable snacks.

Vegetable samosas

Serves 2

Pastry:
225g (8oz) plain flour

1/2 tsp baking powder

1/2 tsp salt

55g (2oz) butter

2-3 tsp yoghurt

Filling:

1 potato, diced

1 carrot, diced

115g (4oz) peas

1 small onion, finely diced

1 garlic clove, diced

1/2 tsp ground ginger

2 green chillies, chopped

1 tsp coriander

1 tsp garam masala

2-3 tbsp stock

Oil or ghee

To season:
Salt and pepper

1 To make the filling, fry the onion, garlic and spices in the oil or ghee until soft.

2 Add the vegetables, stock and seasoning and cook for about 20 minutes.

3 To make the pastry, combine the dry ingredients in a bowl and rub in the butter. Add enough yoghurt to make a firm dough that you can then form into a ball.

4 Knead until smooth and then cover and chill for 30 minutes.

5 Divide the pastry into small balls and then roll them out into a circle about 15cm (6") wide. Cut each in half to give a number of semi-circles.

6 Brush the edges with water or beaten egg yolk and curl each semi-circle into a cone, sealing the edges well.

7 Spoon in some vegetable mixture and then seal well to close.

8 Deep-fry the samosas until crisp and brown and drain them on kitchen paper.

Spinach pakora

Serves 2

115g (4oz) gram flour / self-raising flour

1-2 tsp mixed curry spices, e.g. ground coriander, chilli, cumin and ginger

225g (8oz) spinach, chopped

Salt to taste

Oil or ghee

1 Mix the flour, salt and spices together and slowly add enough water to make a coating batter.

2 Combine the spinach with the batter and then fry spoonfuls in oil or ghee until crisp.

3 If you want to use other vegetables, cut them into bite-sized pieces and dip them in the batter before frying.

4 Drain on kitchen paper before serving.

ROAST VEGETABLES

Roasted vegetables taste juicy and full of flavour. For most vegetables, prepare them by peeling, removing the core or seeds, and halving or cutting into wedges (with beetroot it is easier to roast them whole, then gently remove the skin before they are served). You can either place the vegetables directly in an oiled baking dish and drizzle over olive oil, or first turn them in oil in a bowl to make sure they are well coated. Season well and sprinkle with herbs such as rosemary or thyme. For extra heat, you could add chilli powder, cayenne pepper or paprika.

Bake at 180°C (360°F / Gas Mark 4) for 20-40 minutes, depending on the size of vegetable, and baste with a little of the juices or more oil to make sure they don't dry out.

Roast carrots

When roasting meat, add sliced carrots and other root vegetables to the dish and place them underneath the joint to catch the fat. Unless there is a large amount of meat juice in the pan, add the vegetables half an hour before serving so that they aren't in the oven for too long.

Roast winter squash

Leave the slices unpeeled (as peeling squash can be difficult once the skin has hardened) and eat the flesh directly, or scrape it off and liquidise for soup or other recipes. (Most of the skin might be soft enough to eat but you will find that the sharp corners remain too tough.)

Roast ratatouille

Courgettes, tomatoes, garlic cloves, red onions and red peppers roasted together make a lovely ratatouille-like mixture.

Aubergine and tomato bake

This dish, known in southern Italy as melanzane alla parmigiana, can either be a vegetable dish or a light lunch. It is made with aubergines, cheese and tomato sauce.

Serves 2

1-2 aubergines

285ml (10fl oz / 1/2 pint) tomato sauce (see page 227)

Salt

Olive oil

115g (4oz) cheese, e.g. mozzarella, Parmesan or Cheddar, grated

1   Slice each aubergine vertically into 4-8 pieces and scoop out the seeds. To remove any bitter taste, salt the slices, leave to drain in a colander for 30 minutes and then rinse and dry well.

2   Brush with olive oil and bake at 200°C (400°F / Gas Mark 6) for about 20 minutes, turning once or twice.

3   Grease a baking tin and spoon in a little tomato sauce.

4   Lay half the aubergine slices on top and cover with half the cheese.

5   Cover with more tomato sauce, add another layer of aubergines and then finish with a layer of tomato sauce topped with cheese.

6   Bake for 30 minutes or until the aubergine is soft and the top golden brown.

Vegetable crisps

Vegetables that work well as crisps include beetroot, carrots and even radishes. You can fry thin slices of peeled vegetables quickly in hot oil or, for a healthy snack, don't deep-fry but bake in the oven instead.

Baked vegetable crisps

1   Wash, peel and slice the vegetables very thinly.

2   Place the slices in a bowl with 2 tsp vegetable or olive oil, season with pepper and turn to coat the vegetables well.

3   Lay on baking trays and bake for 10-20 minutes at 200°C (400°F / Gas Mark 6), turning them halfway through.

4   Serve with added salt to taste.

Chapter 5
Main meals

VEGETABLE DISHES

Stuffed vegetables

Tarts, pies and pasties

Pasta

Curry

Rice and grains

Pancakes

Omelettes

Vegetables and cheese

Stir fries

Vegetable burgers

Falafel

Soufflés

Pizza

Casseroles

MEAT AND FISH DISHES

Meat

Fish

VEGETABLE DISHES

You don't have to be a vegetarian to enjoy a vegetable dish, and there is a huge range of no-meat, no-fish recipes that are both satisfying and inexpensive. For many of the recipes included here there are also suggestions for how to make them more attractive to meat eaters.

Stuffed vegetables

The best vegetables for stuffing are those that can be hollowed out, that bake well, keep their shape and have a good ratio of flesh to filling. In the UK the most common vegetables that are served stuffed are red and green peppers, marrow, courgette, squash, aubergines, mushrooms, onions and tomatoes. Winter squash are probably better baked, but you can also cook most stuffed vegetables in liquid such as water or tomato juice on the hob.

Fillings may contain only chopped vegetables mixed together with cheese, ham or bacon and herbs and spices, or you can make a more substantial meal by including some carbohydrate. The two main types normally used for stuffing are rice (common in Middle Eastern cookery) and breadcrumbs (more popular in Europe).

Although you may see recipes using raw rice to stuff vegetables that are to be stewed, I still prefer to cook the rice first to ensure that, if there isn't quite enough liquid, the final dish won't contain hard grains of uncooked rice. The stuffing needs to be very well flavoured, or you will end up with a rather bland dish. Add nuts, dried fruit, cheese or extra herbs and spices to the basic mix for variety.

As well as the recipes that follow, you could stuff your vegetables with pork sausage meat seasoned with sage or apple, or serve them with a cheese or mustard sauce.

Rice stuffing

Serves 2

55-85g (2-3oz) weight raw rice, cooked

1 medium onion, finely chopped

1 garlic clove, crushed

2 tbsp oil

3 tbsp parsley, chopped

1 tsp cinnamon, ground

1 tomato, chopped

1 tsp mint, chopped

Parmesan cheese, grated

Optional: Sultanas; Pine nuts, toasted

170g (6oz) minced lamb/pork/beef

1 tsp coriander/cumin, ground

To season: Salt and pepper

1 Fry the onion and garlic gently in the oil. Add any meat and ground spices (if using) and cook for a further 10 minutes.

2 Cool and then mix with all the other ingredients, including sultanas and pine nuts if you wish.

3 Season and make sure everything is thoroughly blended.

Simple bacon and rice stuffing

Serves 2

1 onion, finely diced

4-6 bacon rashers, chopped

Olive oil

55-85g (2-3oz) weight raw rice, cooked

Basil leaves, chopped

To season: Salt and pepper

1 Sauté the bacon and onion in the oil for 5 minutes.

2 Remove from the heat and stir in the rice and basil.

3 Season well.

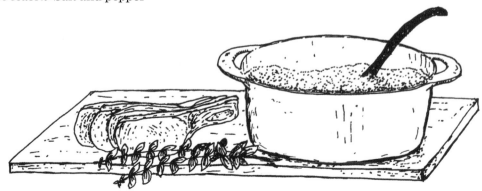

Breadcrumb stuffing

Serves 2

Breadcrumbs made from several slices of day-old bread

1 onion, chopped

1 garlic clove, finely chopped

Herbs, e.g. parsley, oregano or marjoram, chopped

30-55g (1-2oz) cheese, e.g. Parmesan, mozzarella or Cheddar, grated

A little lemon juice

Optional: 170g (6oz) minced meat (optional)

To season: Salt and pepper

To prepare the stuffing:

1   Gently fry the onion and garlic in the oil until soft. Include any meat at this stage and cook for a further 5-10 minutes.

2   Add breadcrumbs to the chopped herbs, cheese and lemon juice.

3   Mix and season well.

To prepare stuffed vegetables:

1   Wash the vegetables and halve courgettes or squash, if using. Scoop out the seeds and some of the flesh and, if appropriate (for example, when stuffing a marrow), divide up large specimens into portion-sized pieces. Try not to pierce the vegetable wall.

2   For very watery vegetables, salt and leave to drain for half an hour before rinsing and drying.

3   For large or thick-skinned vegetables, you can start off the process by simmering or baking them in the oven for 10-15 minutes first, or peel to remove tough skin.

4   Fill the cavities with stuffing. You could add some of the scooped-out vegetable flesh when stuffing tomatoes or courgettes.

5   Stand or lay the vegetables in an oiled baking tin. Drizzle with oil, add a little water to the pan and sprinkle with extra Parmesan or mozzarella.

6   Cover with foil and bake for 30-50 minutes at 180°C (360°F / Gas Mark 4), depending on the size of the vegetables.

7   Remove the foil and bake for an extra 10 minutes if you want a crispy topping – but take care not to dry out any rice too much. (You could add extra cheese at this stage to melt over the filling.)

✳ When using a rice stuffing, you can stew the stuffed vegetables instead. Pack them together in a saucepan. Mix 140ml (5fl oz / 1/4 pint) water with some olive oil and lemon juice (or use tomato juice) and pour this around the vegetables. Simmer, covered, for about 1 hour.

Tarts, pies and pasties

Pastry is a filling carbohydrate to include in a meal, and you can use any combination of vegetables, cheese, eggs and meat to create flans, tarts, quiches, pies or pasties. Some popular vegetable fillings include:

- spinach, curd, Parmesan and Gruyère cheese (börek)
- tomatoes, anchovies and onions (pissaladière)
- tomatoes, Gruyère or Cheddar and cream
- carrots, courgettes and Cheddar
- radishes, cheese and cream
- roasted peppers, tomatoes, aubergine and courgettes. (Mediterranean)

Pastry

Although pies and flans are normally made with puff or shortcrust pastry, you can create more delicate dishes if you use sheets of buttered filo pastry. These can be stacked together to form crispy layers, baked in moulds to create cups, or rolled into little parcels.

Shortcrust pastry

Many people have a favourite pastry recipe, but this is the recipe I tend to use. If you don't make pastry very often, it's a good one to start with. Although it suggests using butter, you may prefer to use margarine, or half lard and half butter.

Before baking, brush the pastry with milk or egg for a golden crust.

225g (8oz) plain flour

140g (5oz) butter

1-2 tbsp cold water / milk

1 Use a fork or your fingers to mix the butter into the flour until it has a crumbly texture.

2 Slowly add water and keep mixing until the pastry forms a soft ball.

3 Use your hands to bring the pastry mix together but do not over-knead.

4 Store in a plastic bag in the fridge for 30 minutes to rest before rolling.

5 When ready to make the pie, flour the surface and roll out the pastry to a thickness of about 0.5cm (1/4").

Or:

To make it easy to work with, roll the pastry out between two layers of cling film – you won't need to flour the surfaces and the rolling pin won't stick to the dough.

To create the dish, peel off the top layer of film, lift and then turn it over to lay the pastry (still on its film base) over the dish. Finally, gently peel away the bottom layer of film.

Baking blind

Many open tarts and flans need to be baked blind to crisp the pastry shell before it is filled. This will prevent the filling from leaking through and ruining the base.

To bake blind, cover the pastry case with greaseproof paper or foil, pour in dried beans or rice that will hold down the paper and stop the pastry becoming distorted, and bake at around 200°C (400°F / Gas Mark 6) for 10-15 minutes.

Once the base is crisp, you can add layers of fried onions, sliced tomatoes or roasted vegetables or fill the pastry case directly with egg custard, cheese or other ingredients and finish it off in the oven.

Deep vegetable pie

Serves 2-3

225-340g (8-12oz) chopped vegetables, e.g. carrots, beans, peas, courgettes, beetroot or mushrooms

1 onion, sliced

1 garlic clove, chopped

Oil for frying

Chopped herbs, e.g. rosemary or thyme

3 tbsp soy sauce

2 tbsp balsamic vinegar

140ml (5fl oz / 1/4 pint) stock

225g (8oz) puff pastry

Milk / egg, beaten

To season: Salt and pepper

You will also need: Deep pie dish

1 Fry the onions and garlic in the oil for 3-4 minutes.

2 Add the rest of the vegetables, herbs, some of the stock, soy sauce and balsamic vinegar and continue cooking for 10-15 minutes. Add extra stock to prevent it from burning.

3 Season well and then transfer the vegetables to a deep pie dish. Include a little of the cooking liquid.

4 Place a support in the dish and then cover with pastry. Roll out the pastry 0.5cm (1/4") thick and make the circle 2cm (3/4") wider than the width of the dish. Cut round the edge of the pastry and use this outer strip to line the wetted rim of the dish before laying the rest of the pastry on top, sealing the edges well.

5 Brush the lid with milk or beaten egg and make small holes in it to let out the steam.

6 Bake at 220°C (430°F / Gas Mark 7) for 10 minutes until the pastry has started to rise and turn golden and then lower the temperature to 190-200°C (380-400°F / Gas Mark 5-6) and bake for a further 30-40 minutes.

Pissaladière

Serves 2-3

1 small onion, finely chopped

2 garlic cloves, finely chopped

Shortcrust pastry made with 225g (8oz) flour

450g (1lb) tomatoes, sliced thickly

1 tbsp dried oregano / other Mediterranean herbs

55g (2oz) Parmesan cheese, grated

85g (3oz) jar anchovy fillets, drained

Handful of black olives, halved and pitted

Olive oil

To season: Salt and pepper

You will also need:
Flan dish

1. Gently cook the garlic and onion for 10 minutes in a little olive oil until soft.
2. Roll out the pastry and line a square or circular flan dish.
3. Prick the base and then bake blind for 15 minutes. Remove the tin and lower the temperature to about 180°C (360°F / Gas Mark 4).
4. Spread the garlic and onions over the base of the pastry.
5. Arrange the tomatoes on top.
6. Sprinkle over the herbs, cheese and seasoning.
7. Make a lattice pattern with the anchovy fillets.
8. Fill the spaces with the halved olives.
9. Drizzle with oil and return to the oven. Continue cooking for a further 15-20 minutes or until the pastry is crisp.

Tomato and cheese tart

Serves 2-3

255g (9oz) puff pastry

4-6 tomatoes, sliced

2 tbsp pesto

200g (7oz) soft cheese, e.g. mozzarella or goat's cheese

Thyme/basil, fresh

To season: Salt and pepper

To serve: Rocket leaves

1. Roll out the pastry and use it to line a greased baking tin.
2. Score round the edge so that it will form a lip as it cooks.
3. Spread pesto over the pastry base and then cover with sliced cheese.
4. Top with the tomatoes and scatter over some thyme or torn basil.
5. Season well and bake at 200°C (400°F / Gas Mark 6) for 25-30 minutes.
6. Pile rocket leaves on top to serve.

Spinach börek

Serves 2-3

30g (1oz) butter

1 onion / 2-3 spring onions, chopped

680g (1lb 8oz) spinach, cooked, drained, chopped

285g (10oz) cheese, e.g. curd, grated Gruyère, Parmesan or crumbled feta

140ml (5fl oz / 1/4 pint) double cream

3 eggs

Pinch of nutmeg

450g (1lb) filo pastry

Melted butter

To season: Salt and pepper

1 Melt the butter, gently fry the onion for a few minutes and then add the spinach.

2 Cook for another 5 minutes.

3 Remove from the heat and beat in the cheeses, eggs and cream.

4 Season and add the nutmeg.

5 Take sheets of filo pastry, cut them into 8cm (3") wide strips and brush with melted butter.

6 Place a teaspoonful of filling near the end of each strip and roll up to completely enclose the filling.

7 Brush all the parcels with melted butter and bake at 200°C (400°F / Gas Mark 6) for 20-30 minutes until brown and crisp.

✳ As an alternative, make a single spinach and cheese tart by lining a flan dish with several layers of pastry, each one brushed with butter, and then adding the filling.

Quick flan or quiche

Serves 2-3

Shortcrust pastry made using 225g (8oz) flour

140g-170g (5-6oz) vegetables (pre-cook root vegetables, mushrooms or onions)

2 eggs

140ml (5fl oz / 1/4 pint) milk

115-170g (4-6oz) cheese, e.g. Cheddar, grated

4 tbsp yoghurt / crème fraiche

Parmesan cheese, grated

Optional:
Herbs, grilled bacon, ham or cooked chicken

To season: Salt and pepper

1. Line a greased flan tin with pastry and bake blind at a high temperature (see page 91) .
2. Lower the oven temperature to 180°C (360°F / Gas Mark 4) and remove the tin.
3. Arrange a good layer of vegetables in the bottom of the pastry case and add any herbs or meat if included.
4. Whisk the eggs, cheese and milk together and stir in enough yoghurt / crème fraiche to give a thick custard.
5. Season well and pour into the pastry case.
6. Sprinkle Parmesan over the top and then return to the oven and continue cooking for a further 20-30 minutes until the centre is firm and any raw vegetables are cooked.

Cheese pastry flan

Serves 2-3

170g (6oz) vegetables, e.g. carrots, radishes or tomatoes, chopped/sliced

115g (4oz) plain flour

55g (2oz) butter

115g (4oz) cheese e.g. Cheddar, Gouda or Gruyère, grated

225ml (8fl oz) cream or yoghurt

2 large eggs

1/4 tsp salt

Optional:
170g (6oz) cream cheese or ricotta

You will also need: Pie dish

1. Make cheese pastry by cutting the butter into the flour and mixing in half the cheese and 55ml (2fl oz) cream or yoghurt. Chill for half an hour before using.
2. Line a pie dish with the pastry and bake blind for 10-12 minutes at a high temperature (see page 91). Remove from the oven and lower the oven temperature to 190°C (380°F / Gas Mark 5).
3. Sprinkle the rest of the cheese over the pastry base.
4. Add the sliced vegetables. If they will take time to cook, then fry, steam or stew them lightly first.
5. Mix the rest of the cream or yoghurt with the eggs and salt and pour into the dish to cover the vegetables. (You could replace the cream or yoghurt with 170g [6oz] cream cheese or ricotta.)
6. Return to the oven and bake for 20-25 minutes.

Pasta

Nowadays you can buy both dried and fresh pasta, but some dishes such as ravioli are still more fun if you make your own dough. If you can, buy Italian type 00 flour, which is finer than normal flour.

Either use a pasta machine to roll out the dough, taking it from the widest to narrowest setting a number of times, or roll it with a rolling pin on a floured surface.

The recommended portions are 85-115g (3-4oz) dried pasta per person.

For filled pasta such as ravioli or cannelloni, try:
* ricotta and cooked, chopped spinach
* ricotta and puréed butternut squash with nutmeg
* puréed peas with garlic, crème fraiche and mint.

Pasta dough

Makes 2 portions

200g (7oz) plain flour

1/2 tsp salt

2 eggs

Olive oil

1 Mix together the flour and salt and make a well in the centre of the bowl.

2 Stir in the eggs and start blending the mixture, adding a little oil and water if necessary to form a smooth dough.

3 Knead the dough on a floured surface for about 5 minutes.

4 Wrap the dough in cling film and rest it in the fridge for at least half an hour.

5 On a floured surface, roll out the dough very thinly – for example, to 0.15cm (1/8") thickness. (If the single ball of dough is difficult to work with, divide it into 4 or 6 pieces and roll each of these separately.)

6 Cut the dough into sheets or ribbons, or use strips to make stuffed ravioli.

7 If using fresh pasta, it will take only 3-5 minutes rather than 10-15 minutes to cook.

Vegetable sauce for pasta

As well as stirring vegetables through the pasta, you can make more of a dish by combining finely diced vegetables with cheese and other dairy products and mixing or blending them together into a thick creamy sauce.

Serves 3-4

2-3 tomatoes, sliced

3 small courgettes, sliced

7-8 runner beans / green beans, chopped

1 tbsp olive oil

1/2 tbsp butter

100ml (3 1/2 fl oz) crème fraiche / plain yoghurt

55g (2oz) Parmesan, grated

Salt and pepper

Optional: 100g (3 1/2 oz) tinned pulses or other vegetables

1 Gently fry the tomatoes and courgettes in the oil and butter for a few minutes.

2 Add the runner beans or green beans and cook for 5-8 minutes. You could also add pulses or other vegetables at the same time as the runner/green beans.

3 Stir in the crème fraiche / yoghurt and cheese.

4 Season and either leave whole or blend for a smoother sauce.

Use up green or runner beans in a healthy pasta sauce.

Pasta with broad beans

Serves 2-3

Pasta, e.g. fettuccine

140g (5oz) broad beans, cooked

1 tbsp olive oil

1 garlic clove, crushed

115g (4oz) mozzarella, chopped

2 tbsp oregano, fresh, chopped

To season: Salt and pepper

To serve:
Parmesan cheese, grated

1 Cook the pasta for 5-10 minutes until al dente, i.e. it still has a bite.

2 Drain and return to the pan off the heat.

3 Stir in the rest of the ingredients immediately so that the cheese just starts to melt into the hot pasta.

4 Season and serve with Parmesan cheese and black pepper.

Bolognese

This classic dish uses minced beef or lamb with tomatoes, but you can substitute the meat with lentils, carrots and/or mushrooms to make an alternative vegetarian dish.

Serves 4

Pasta, e.g. spaghetti

340g (12oz) minced meat

1 onion, chopped

1 garlic clove, diced

1 tbsp tomato purée

6 large tomatoes, chopped

Olive oil

1/2 glass red wine

2 bay leaves

1 tsp dried thyme

Stock as required

To season: Salt and pepper

To serve:
Parmesan cheese, grated

1 Fry the onion and garlic in the oil for a couple of minutes.

2 Add the meat and brown for about 5 minutes.

3 Add the tomato purée, tomatoes, wine and herbs and bring to the boil.

4 Simmer for about 20-25 minutes, adding extra stock if required.

5 Season well and remove the bay leaves.

6 Cook the pasta for 8-10 minutes and serve with the bolognese sauce and grated cheese.

Spinach lasagne

Traditional lasagne involves layering sheets of pasta with bolognese sauce, cheese sauce and grated cheese, finishing with a topping of white or cheese sauce. This recipe is a good alternative when you want to use up some spinach.

Serves 4

6-8 sheets fresh lasagne / dried, 'no pre-cook' lasagne

450g (1lb) spinach, fresh

Cheese sauce made with 200ml (7fl oz) milk (see page 107)

225ml (8fl oz) tomato sauce (see page 227)

170g (6oz) ricotta cheese

55g (2oz) Parmesan cheese, grated

115g (4oz) mozzarella cheese, grated

30g (1oz) butter

Pinch of nutmeg

✳ For a lighter dish, replace the sheets of lasagne with cooked pancakes. You could also roll up pancakes stuffed with the spinach and cheese mixture, cover them in cheese and tomato sauce and serve these as an alternative to cannelloni.

---

1 Cook the spinach in the butter, drain and then squeeze out all the water. Chop and blend with the ricotta and half the cheese sauce. Season with a little nutmeg.

2 In a large ovenproof dish, spoon in a quarter of the tomato sauce and then cover this with a layer of lasagne, tearing this into pieces to fit the dish.

3 Top with some of the spinach mixture.

4 Add another layer of lasagne and then some of the plain cheese sauce sprinkled with mozzarella.

5 Add a layer of lasagne and cover this with more tomato sauce.

6 Repeat the layers to use up all the spinach and cheese sauce, finishing with a layer of lasagne.

7 Cover this with the last spoonfuls of tomato sauce and sprinkle on Parmesan and mozzarella.

8 Bake at 180°C (360°F / Gas Mark 40 for about 40 minutes.

Pasticcio

If you don't have lasagne or pancakes, you can still make a layered pasta dish. Replace the sheets of lasagne with cooked pasta shapes such as penne or fusilli, and then either use layers of bolognese and cheese sauce or create a spinach and ricotta dish as suggested above.

Curry

Although there are lots of curry sauces on the market that you can stir vegetables into, it is much more satisfying to make a curry from scratch. I like to use jars of spices such as crushed chillies and ginger which can be combined with the water or stock, but when using any powdered or whole spices you need to fry them for a few minutes before adding the liquid ingredients so that your final dish doesn't taste powdery and the full flavour is released.

Most vegetables, including carrots, courgettes, beetroot, beans, peas and squash, can be added to this curry, but you may want to balance out those with strong flavours so they do not dominate the finished dish. To preserve their colour, only add the tomatoes near the end of the cooking time.

In earlier times, curries were often made with apples and raisins and you may like to try this for a change, but this type of 'English' curry is not very popular nowadays.

If you like curried chicken, try this delicious spinach and yoghurt curry (see page 122).

Vegetable curry

Serves 4

255g (9oz) mixed vegetables, chopped

3-4 large tomatoes, chopped

1 onion, chopped

1 garlic clove, crushed

Oil

2 tsp chillies, crushed / chilli powder / hot chilli, chopped

2 tsp ginger, crushed/ground

2 tsp turmeric, ground

2 tsp coriander, ground

2 tsp cumin, ground

2 tsp cardamom, ground

140ml (5fl oz / 1/4 pint) stock

To season:
Salt and pepper

To garnish:
Coriander, fresh

To serve:
Rice and/or naan bread

Cucumber and yoghurt raita

1   Fry the onion in the oil for a few minutes until transparent.

2   Add the dry spices and garlic and fry for 2-3 minutes.

3   Add the vegetables, apart from the tomatoes, and any fresh spices, reducing the amount of chilli for those who do not like hot curries, and fry for a further 5 minutes.

4   Add the stock, bring to the boil and then simmer for 20-30 minutes. Only add extra liquid if there is a danger it will dry out, as you should aim for a thick consistency.

5   Add the tomatoes and cook for a final 5 minutes.

6   Season well, garnish with coriander and serve with rice and/or naan bread and cucumber and yoghurt dip (raita) (see page 230).

Rice and grains

Many countries have special rice dishes and these include Spanish paella, Italian risotto and Indian pulao or pilaf. Although you can simply mix vegetables with cooked rice as a quick way to use up leftovers, dishes where the rice is cooked along with the vegetables will have a much fuller flavour.

Risotto involves frying vegetables, meat or seafood together with slow-cooked Arborio or risotto rice. This rice has smaller grains than ordinary rice and is cooked in a frying pan. Stock is added a little at a time rather than all at once at the beginning of cooking, which allows time for liquid to be completely absorbed before more is added. This process continues until the rice is just cooked. The dish is moist and creamy and is often served with grated Parmesan cheese. In UK restaurants, the two most common types of vegetable risotto you will be offered are butternut squash and mushroom.

Pilaf is made with basmati or long grain rice and involves mixing lightly cooked vegetables with rice and stock, then simmering or baking them together until the rice is cooked.

For a change from rice, you can also create filling meals using couscous or bulgur wheat. To cook these grains, either simmer them for 10-15 minutes in water, or place them in a bowl, pour in enough boiling water to cover, and leave for 10-15 minutes to allow the grains to absorb all the liquid, before draining and serving.

Vegetable risotto

Serves 3

200g (7oz) Arborio (risotto) rice

1 small butternut squash, sliced, or 255g (9oz) chopped vegetables, e.g. mushrooms, sliced green beans, carrots, courgettes, peas or skinned broad beans

1 tbsp olive oil / butter

1 onion, diced

1 garlic clove, diced

1 small glass white wine

Herbs, e.g. thyme

850ml (30fl oz / 1½ pints) vegetable stock

Lemon juice

Parmesan cheese

Optional:
Crème fraiche

Chicken livers, chopped / prawns / chicken / bacon

To season: Salt and pepper

To garnish: Herbs / pea shoots

1 If using squash, first season the slices, coat them in olive oil and bake in the oven at 180°C (360°F / Gas Mark 4) for 40-50 minutes. Cool and then scrape off and mash the flesh.

2 Gently fry the garlic and onion in the oil or butter until transparent but not coloured.

3 Add any raw vegetables to the pan and cook for a further 5 minutes. (For a more substantial dish, you can add chopped chicken livers, prawns, chicken or bacon at this point.)

4 Add the rice and stir until well coated with oil.

5 Add the white wine and herbs, cover and cook gently for 4-5 minutes until almost dry.

6 Add a quarter of the stock, stir well and simmer uncovered until almost evaporated.

7 Repeat adding stock until the rice is just cooked but still has a slight bite. You may not need it all.

8 Stir in any cooked vegetables or squash, season well, add a little lemon juice and heat through for a few minutes.

9 Stir in the Parmesan, garnish with fresh herbs and pea shoots and serve. You could also add some crème fraiche for extra creaminess.

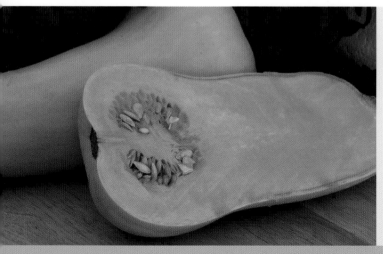

One of the most popular risottos served in UK restaurants is made with butternut squash.

Broad beans and bulgur wheat

Personally I find that couscous, with its small grains, easily becomes mushy, so I tend to cook only bulgur wheat, but either are fine for this recipe.

Serves 2

200g (7oz) broad beans, podded

3-4 tomatoes, chopped

1 onion, chopped

1 garlic clove, chopped

140g (5oz) bulgur wheat

1/2 red pepper, chopped

285ml (10fl oz / 1/2 pint) stock

Olive oil

To season: Salt and pepper

To garnish: Coriander, fresh, chopped

1 Fry the onion in the oil for a few minutes until transparent, add the garlic and then fry for a few more minutes.

2 Add the rest of the ingredients, including most of the stock, and simmer gently for about 10-15 minutes, adding more stock if the mixture starts to dry out.

3 Season well and garnish with coriander.

Vegetable pilaf

Use any mix of vegetables you have for this dish. For a different flavour, fry 115g (4oz) diced bacon before adding the vegetables. For a more authentic Indian dish, fry some ground cloves, cinnamon, cardamom, chopped chillies and ginger with the vegetables or include whole curry spices with the rice.

Serves 2-3

1 onion, diced

2 garlic cloves, crushed

340g (12oz) mixed vegetables, e.g. butternut squash, peas, carrots, courgettes and red peppers, diced

170g (6oz) basmati rice

425ml (15fl oz / 3/4 pint) water/stock

Olive oil

To season: Salt and pepper

To garnish: 2-3 tbsp parsley/coriander, chopped

1 Gently fry the onion for a few minutes in the oil.

2 Add the rest of the vegetables and fry for 5 minutes.

3 Add the rice and cook for 2-3 minutes until it starts to become transparent.

4 Stir in the stock, season and simmer for 20-30 minutes or transfer to an ovenproof dish, cover with a lid or foil and bake at 200°C (400°F / Gas Mark 6) for 30-35 minutes.

5 Scatter with the parsley or coriander and serve.

Pancakes

Normally when making pancakes you add a filling of previously cooked vegetables and fold over half the pancake just before serving. For a more substantial dish, you can roll up several filled pancakes, pack them closely together in a baking dish and pour over cheese sauce (see page 107). Bake for 20 minutes until the sauce is brown and bubbling.

Any vegetables can be used as a pancake stuffing, including spinach, courgettes, green beans, sweetcorn, carrots, peppers, peas, onions, mushrooms and tomatoes. You can also include ham and bacon or cheese such as feta, Cheddar or Gruyère for a more substantial dish.

Stuffed pancakes

Serves 2

Batter:

1 egg

100g (3 1/2 oz) plain flour

140ml (5fl oz / 1/4 pint) milk

Filling:

1/2 onion, sliced

Mixed vegetables, e.g. courgettes, beetroot, green beans, broad beans or peas, diced

Herbs, e.g. parsley, chopped

Oil for frying

To season: Salt and pepper

To garnish:
Herbs, e.g. parsley, chopped

Cheese, grated

1   Make the batter by beating the egg and slowly stirring it into the flour. Start adding the milk, stirring well, until the batter is the consistency of thin cream.

2   To prepare the filling, heat some oil and fry the vegetables for 5-10 minutes or steam them instead. Season well and stir in a handful of herbs.

3   To cook the pancakes, heat oil in a clean frying pan and pour in enough batter to coat the base.

4   Cook for a couple of minutes, flip over and then cook the other side.

5   Turn out on to a warmed plate.

6   Spoon vegetable filling on to one half of the pancake, fold over the other half and garnish with more herbs and perhaps some cheese.

Omelettes

For omelettes, either cook the eggs and add the vegetables at the last minute, or cook the eggs and vegetables together from the start. If you make a thicker frittata or a tortilla, where the eggs are cooked for some time, it can be served cut into slices and is good to eat cold.

For a fluffy omelette, separate the eggs and whisk the egg whites before stirring into the beaten yolks. For a more solid dish, fry any vegetables and then add the egg mixture to the vegetables left in the pan and cook them together, turning the omelette over halfway through to cook both sides. Add the cheese just before serving.

Courgette omelette

1-2 small courgettes, finely sliced

2 eggs per person

Butter or oil

30g (1oz) Cheddar/ricotta cheese, broken up

Herbs, e.g. chopped basil or thyme

To season: Salt and pepper

1. Brown the courgettes in hot oil or butter and then remove from the pan.

2. Beat the eggs lightly, season well and start frying in the hot fat. Lift the edges of the omelette so that uncooked egg is allowed to run out and start to set.

3. After a couple of minutes, when the omelette is almost ready, scatter over the cooked courgettes, herbs and cheese.

4. Cook for another minute and then fold half the omelette over on itself.

5. Remove from the heat – the cheese will continue to melt inside the warm omelette as you serve the dish.

Tortilla (Spanish omelette)

Although traditionally made with just potatoes and onions, this recipe is ideal for using up cooked, chopped vegetables such as peas, carrots, courgettes, beetroot or green beans.

Serves 2

1 or 2 large potato(es), sliced/cubed, salted

1/2 onion, finely chopped

3 eggs

285-340g (10-12oz) vegetables, cooked

Olive oil

Salt

1 Fry the potatoes gently in the oil. Stir regularly so they do not brown or stick to the pan. (If you are in a hurry, pre-cook the potatoes.)

2 After 5 minutes, stir the onion into the pan and continue cooking and turning until the potatoes are just starting to break up.

3 Beat the eggs in a bowl with a little salt and add the vegetables together with the hot potato mixture.

4 Return them all to the pan – possibly using a clean pan and/or first adding a little extra oil and waiting for the pan to heat up.

5 Press down the mixture and leave to continue cooking on a medium heat for 10 minutes.

6 Using a plate held over the mixture, turn it over and return it to the pan to cook the other side.

7 Cook for a further 5 minutes before serving in slices.

Vegetable frittata

Serves 2

Mixed vegetables, e.g. carrots, peas, courgettes, diced

1 onion, chopped

Olive oil

Herbs, e.g. parsley or thyme, chopped

4 eggs

Salt and pepper

Optional:
Cheese / meat (cooked) to taste

1 Gently fry the onion in the oil for a few minutes.

2 Add the vegetables and herbs and continue cooking for a couple of minutes.

3 Beat the eggs with salt and pepper and either pour into the pan or first mix with the vegetables and any cheese or meat before returning everything to the pan.

4 Cook the mixture, stirring occasionally until the eggs start to set.

5 Make sure everything is thoroughly mixed and then cook gently for a further 2-3 minutes without stirring.

6 Brown the top under the grill or turn out the frittata on to a plate, turn it over and return to the pan to cook the bottom for another minute or so.

Vegetables and cheese

Most vegetables can be baked, and for a substantial dish they are often mixed with a cheese sauce or cooked 'au gratin'. The name comes from the dish originally used for this type of meal and the cooking method involves layering vegetables with cheese or simply using a mixture of grated cheese and vegetables. Some sort of topping is usually added such as breadcrumbs or extra grated cheese so that the finished dish has a crusty top. As an alternative, you can top baked vegetable dishes with a layer of sliced potatoes drizzled with olive oil before adding a final layer of cheese.

You can experiment with a variety of cheeses but mixtures that make excellent gratins include spinach, tomatoes and mozzarella; tomatoes, peppers and goat's cheese; root vegetables and Cheddar cheese; and squash and Gruyère.

Cheese sauce

Serves 2

2 tbsp butter

1½ tbsp plain flour

140ml (5fl oz / ¼ pint) milk

115g (4oz) cheese, e.g. Cheddar or Gruyère, grated

To season: Salt and pepper

1 Melt the butter gently in a pan.

2 Stir in the flour and cook for 1 minute.

3 Slowly start to add the milk, stirring all the time.

4 Continue stirring and adding milk until the sauce has a creamy consistency and then leave it to cook for a few more minutes.

5 Take the pan off the heat, stir in the cheese and season to taste. Do not reheat the sauce, or the cheese will become stringy.

✳ Many people find making smooth sauces difficult, but I have found that the fail-safe way to avoid lumps in a white or cheese sauce is simply to make sure there is always more fat than flour in the pan.

Vegetables in cheese sauce

The most well-known vegetable dish using cheese sauce is cauliflower cheese, but you could combine cheese sauce with other vegetables such as broccoli, courgettes, Brussels sprouts or leeks, or a mixture of these, to make an excellent family supper dish.

Serve using one of the following methods:

- Pour the sauce over the cooked vegetables just before serving.
- Pour the sauce over the raw vegetables in a greased ovenproof dish and then bake for 20-30 minutes at about 180°C (360°F / Gas Mark 4) until the vegetables are soft and the topping is bubbling and brown.
- Place cooked vegetables in a heat-proof dish, coat them in sauce, and then brown the dish under the grill.

Spinach and eggs Florentine style

This classic dish is usually made with Hollandaise sauce, but here is a very simple version using cheese sauce.

Serves 2

115g (4oz) spinach

Butter

2 eggs

Cheese sauce (see page 107)

Optional: Nutmeg

To season: Salt and pepper

You will also need:
Heatproof ramekin dishes

1 Lightly fry or microwave the spinach with butter for a few minutes and stir in nutmeg or just season well.

2 Drain and chop.

3 Poach the eggs.

4 Divide the spinach between greased ramekin dishes.

5 Make an indentation with the back of a spoon in the centre of each one and place a poached egg in it.

6 Cover with cheese sauce and brown under the grill.

Any mix of vegetables can be used for a gratin.

Vegetable gratin

Serves 2

4 large tomatoes, sliced

1 medium onion, sliced

2-3 courgettes, sliced

Other vegetables, e.g. beans, carrots and peppers, chopped

115g (4oz) Parmesan/Cheddar cheese, grated

4 tsp herbs, e.g. parsley, thyme or basil, chopped

2 tbsp olive oil

To season: Salt and pepper

1. Mix all the ingredients together well, using half the cheese, and season.

2. Spread out the mixture in a shallow, oiled, baking dish.

3. Sprinkle on the rest of the cheese as a topping.

4. Cover with foil pierced in a few places to release steam. (This will prevent the dish from drying out too quickly before everything is properly cooked.)

5. Bake for 40 minutes at 180°C (360°F / Gas Mark 4).

6. Take off the foil and finish at 200°C (400°F / Gas Mark 6) for a further 10-15 minutes until the cheese is bubbling.

Potato bake

You can quickly make a simple supper dish by combining chopped vegetables such as carrots, peas, broad beans, courgette, beetroot or frozen sweetcorn with mashed potatoes and cheese and baking until the topping is crisp. You could also add grilled bacon or chopped ham.

Serves 2

3 large potatoes, diced, cooked

225g (8oz) mixed vegetables, diced

1 onion / 3-4 spring onions, chopped

Milk

Butter

85g (3oz) Cheddar cheese, grated

Optional: 2-3 rashers grilled bacon or chopped ham

To season: Salt and pepper

1 Mash the potatoes with milk and butter.

2 Lightly cook the vegetables for about 10 minutes.

3 Mix together the mash, drained vegetables, onions or spring onions and any extra items such as diced, grilled rashers of bacon or chopped ham.

4 Season well and turn into a greased baking tin or oven dish.

5 Top with cheese.

6 Bake in the oven at 180°C (360°F / Gas Mark 4) for about half an hour until the topping is brown and crispy.

Stir fries

This is a good way to use up any left-over meat, from a large Sunday roast, for example, but you can also make a satisfying vegetarian stir-fry meal by substituting mushrooms or pulses such as kidney beans. Alternatively, cook fresh prawns, diced chicken or beef strips as you create the dish. If you have a wok it will cut the cooking times, but an ordinary frying pan is fine and you should be able to prepare it in about 15 minutes.

The essence of a stir fry is to cook bite-sized pieces in a little oil at high temperatures, and to add ingredients in the right order so that those needing the longest cooking time start frying first. I much prefer using the 'straight to wok'-style noodles as you can add them at the last minute, but if you prefer dried egg noodles, cook them according to the instructions first and drain before adding.

As long as they are cut up finely, you can introduce practically any vegetables, including carrots, peas, lettuce, squash, courgette and all types of bean, as well as red pepper, sweetcorn and Chinese cabbage. But for an authentic taste you may like to add beansprouts and perhaps bamboo shoots or chopped water chestnuts.

Basic stir fry

Serves 2-3

1 onion, diced

1 garlic clove, crushed

85-115g (3-4oz) raw meat per person, diced (or equivalent left-over cooked meat)

225g (8oz) mixed vegetables, diced

3-4 tbsp dark soy sauce

1 tsp Chinese five spice

1-2 tsp fresh root ginger, ground/diced

Gravy / small glass of dry sherry / water / stock

1 pack instant noodles per person

Oil, e.g. peanut, sesame or vegetable

Optional: 1/2 tsp lemongrass

To garnish: Coriander, fresh

1   Heat a little oil in the pan until it is very hot and then quickly fry the onion for a minute.

2   If cooking raw meat, add this now and cook for 2-3 minutes.

3   Add the vegetables, garlic and spices and cook these for 3-4 minutes. If using bean sprouts, add these a little later as they need very little cooking.

4   Add the soy sauce and, after a few minutes, stir in enough gravy/sherry/stock to give a rich sauce whilst not letting the meal become watery.

5   Leave to cook for a couple of minutes.

6   Add any cooked meat now – not earlier or it may become tough.

7   Stir in the cooked or instant noodles making sure they are well coated. Cook for a couple of minutes.

8   Serve. You can garnish each plate with coriander if you wish.

Vegetable burgers

Grilled or fried vegetable (veggie) burgers make a substantial meal and can be made using a wide range of vegetables and pulses. The vegetables may be lightly cooked first and either very finely diced or grated, although you could also blend them into a thick purée. You can use egg, mashed potato, cheese, breadcrumbs and/or oats to thicken and bind the vegetables together, and once formed into cakes they can be frozen to cook at a later date.

To cook, either coat the burgers with seasoned flour and shallow-fry or dip them in beaten egg and then breadcrumbs before deep-frying.

Mixed vegetable burgers

Makes approximately 4 burgers

400g (14oz) mixed vegetables e.g. carrots, peas, courgettes and beans, grated/diced

1 large onion, finely chopped

1 garlic clove, finely chopped

1 tsp cumin, ground

1 tsp coriander, ground

2 tbsp fresh coriander/thyme, chopped

1 tbsp olive oil

1 egg, beaten

70g (2 1/2 oz) breadcrumbs

Flour

To season: Salt and pepper

To serve:
Buns; Lettuce; Cucumber; Ketchup

1 Lightly fry the onion, garlic, herbs and spices in the oil.

2 Add the vegetables and cook for 5-10 minutes until soft.

3 Season well and then leave to cool.

4 Stir in the egg and breadcrumbs to form a mixture that holds together well.

5 On a floured plate, shape into 4 burgers.

6 Shallow-fry for about 5 minutes each side until golden brown.

7 Serve as a conventional burger – in a bun with lettuce, cucumber and ketchup.

Falafel

This is a specialised vegetable burger found in Middle Eastern cookery. Although usually based on chickpeas, falafel can be made with other pulses or beans such as broad beans.

Broad bean falafel

Makes 6-8 falafel

115g (4oz) broad beans, podded

55g (2oz) onion, chopped

1 garlic clove, chopped

Handful of parsley and fresh coriander, chopped

1/2 tsp cumin, ground

1/2 tsp salt

3-4 tbsp water

Oil

Optional: Pinch of hot chilli powder or flakes

To serve:
Cucumber and yoghurt dip

1   Simmer the broad beans for 5-10 minutes and then allow to cool. For older beans, remove the skins.

2   Thoroughly blend the beans with all the other ingredients except the water.

3   Add enough water to form a soft but not wet mixture.

4   As the mixture easily fall apart when frying, chill it for 1 hour before cooking.

5   Shallow-fry spoonfuls in hot oil for about 3-4 minutes each side, until they are crisp and brown. They should still be slightly soft in the centre.

6   You could also form the mixture into balls and bake them in the oven for 20 minutes at 180°C (360°F / Gas Mark 4).

7   Serve with a cucumber and yoghurt dip (see page 230).

Soufflés

Soufflés are made by enriching a white sauce with egg yolks and then stirring in any pre-cooked vegetables together with whisked egg whites and other ingredients, such as chopped ham or grated cheese. The mixture is then spooned or poured into an oiled ovenproof dish and baked until the topping is puffed up and golden. Soufflés are ready to eat when they are firm on the outside but still slightly runny inside.

Lettuce/spinach soufflé

Serves 2

225g (8oz) vegetables such as lettuce or spinach, well washed

2 spring onions, chopped

30g (1oz) butter

2 tbsp flour

140ml (5fl oz / 1/4 pint) milk

3 eggs, separated

115g (4oz) Cheddar cheese, grated

1/4 tsp nutmeg

To season: Salt and pepper

1 Cook the spinach, lettuce or other vegetables in a little water for 5 minutes. Drain well. Chop finely.

2 Melt the butter in a separate pan and add the flour and milk to make a white sauce.

3 Allow to cool and then beat in the egg yolks and stir in the cooked vegetables and onions.

4 Season well.

5 Whisk the egg whites until stiff and fold into the mixture together with the cheese.

6 Sprinkle on the nutmeg and bake in an oiled dish at 190°C (380°F / Gas Mark 5) for 30-40 minutes until well risen.

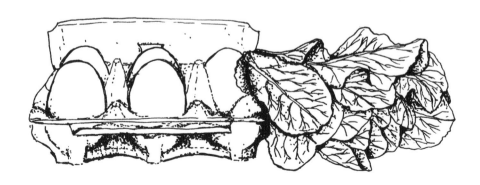

Pizza

It is very easy to prepare pizza dough and need only take about 5 minutes, but you will have to leave it to prove (rise) for 1 or 2 hours before it can be baked. If you want a quicker meal, pizza bases are now readily available in most supermarkets.

Five-minute pizza dough

Makes enough dough for two 31cm (12") bases

680g (1lb 8oz) strong white flour

1 packet (7g/ 1/4 oz) instant dried yeast

2 heaped tsp salt

2 tsp sugar

425ml (15fl oz / 3/4 pint) warm water

1-2 tbsp vegetable oil

1. Mix all the dry ingredients in a bowl.

2. Pour over the oil.

3. Boil a kettle and mix 285ml (10fl oz / 1/2 pint) cold water with 140ml (5fl oz / 1/4 pint) boiling water. This will result in the total amount of water at just the right temperature (hand-hot).

4. Pour the water into the mixture and bring it all together with a large spoon.

5. Knead for 2-3 minutes until it forms a soft dough.

6. Place the bowl of dough inside a plastic bag and leave for 1-2 hours in a warm place until well risen.

7. When you are ready to make the pizzas, divide the dough in half. For each one, squash down the dough ball and then gently press and pull it out with your fingers until you create a disc 30cm (12") in diameter that will fit a greased pizza pan or large tin.

8. Pinch up the edges to hold any runny filling.

9. Cover with the toppings of your choice (see overleaf) and bake at 200°C (400°F / Gas Mark 6) for 20-30 minutes.

Pizza toppings

- Tomato sauce (see page 227) – spread out in a thick layer.

- Cheese – you can use any combination of cheeses such as goat's, Cheddar, feta and mozzarella either grated or broken into small pieces.

- Olives, capers or anchovies.

- Chopped strips of ham, cooked chicken or salami.

- Chopped herbs – e.g. oregano, rosemary, basil or thyme.

- Sliced onions – red, white or spring onions.

- Vegetables such as sweetcorn, chopped spinach, courgettes, red pepper or mushrooms. (Pre-cook if they will take too long or dry out.)

- Olive oil – drizzled over the filling and the edges of the dough.

Alternative pizza ideas

- After adding the topping, fold in half and seal the edges well to create a large calzone (similar-looking to a Cornish pasty).

- Divide the dough into 6-8 pieces, form into balls and flatten before making individual mini-pizzas or folded calzones. Set these well spaced out on an oiled baking tray and bake for 15-20 minutes.

Casseroles

Perhaps the simplest way to cook a number of vegetables is to make a casserole or stew. As long as these are seasoned well, they can be very satisfying as well as healthy, especially if you include a tin of pre-cooked pulses such as chickpeas or butter beans. Serve the casserole with potatoes, dumplings or slices of bread. Alternatively, fry curry spices and chillies with the onions, or add nuts, capers, olives, fresh herbs and slices of tomato stored in oil for a more Mediterranean flavour.

For a more hearty, non-vegetarian meal, nothing beats a sausage casserole, or you could add chicken pieces or stewing lamb. Fry any meat with the onions and make sure it is cooked enough before finishing off the dish.

If you have time, the ideal way to create a casserole – so that each flavour is distinct and no ingredient is overcooked – is to lightly fry the vegetables individually first. You can then fry the onions, add the cooked vegetables and a little stock and seasonings, and heat through before serving. However, for busy cooks just follow the recipe as set out overleaf, ideally staggering the addition of each type of vegetable so that you start with root vegetables or squash and give the least cooking time to those with a higher water content such as courgettes, or anywhere you still want to have 'bite'.

Vegetable casserole with dumplings

Serves 2-3

450g (1lb) of any vegetables – ideally a good mix, e.g. carrots, courgettes, green beans, beetroot, peas, tomatoes, red peppers and squash, peeled and chopped

1 onion, chopped

1 garlic clove, diced

Oil

285-570ml (10-20fl oz / 1/2-1 pint) vegetable stock

1 tbsp tomato purée

1 tbsp Worcester sauce

To season: Salt and pepper

Dumplings:

100g (3 1/2 oz) self-raising flour

50g (1.75oz) shredded suet

1 tsp chopped herbs, e.g. parsley

1/4 tsp salt

1/4 tsp pepper

1 Fry the onions in the oil for a few minutes until transparent.

2 Add any root vegetables and cook for a further 5 minutes.

3 Add the rest of the vegetables and continue to cook for a few more minutes.

4 Add the rest of the ingredients, including half the stock, bring to the boil and then simmer for 20 minutes or so until the vegetables are cooked. Check regularly and add extra stock if necessary, but do not make the casserole too watery.

5 Season well before serving.

6 If you want to include dumplings, place the dry ingredients and herbs in a bowl and stir in enough cold water to make a soft dough. Divide this into small balls and add them to the cooking pot with the stock as they need about 15-20 minutes to cook properly.

The addition of herbs and dumplings can turn the most everyday of vegetables into a delicious casserole.

MEAT AND FISH DISHES

As well as straightforward stews, where carrots, peas, beans or other vegetables are cooked with meat or fish, there are some unusual or particularly tasty combination dishes you might like to try using both vegetables and fruit.

Meat

If you want to cook beef or pork there are a variety of dishes that lend themselves particularly well to the addition of fruit or vegetables. This section also includes a couple of chicken dishes you may not have come across before.

Beef, tomatoes and green/runner beans

In this dish, the beans are not kept al dente – so they will become brown and soft rather than staying crisp and green.

Serves 4

450g (1lb) stewing beef, diced

450g (1lb) green beans, chopped

450g (1lb) tomatoes, puréed or chopped

225g (8oz) potatoes, peeled and chopped

225g (8oz) onions, chopped

1 garlic clove, chopped

2-3 tbsp parsley

Olive oil

To season: Salt and pepper

1 Heat the oil, brown the meat and then add the onions.

2 Fry for a few minutes and then add the garlic.

3 Fry for a further minute and then add the tomatoes and enough water to just cover the meat.

4 Bring to the boil and simmer for about 30-50 minutes.

5 Add the potatoes, beans and parsley and cook for a further 30-40 minutes until the meat is soft and the vegetables are well cooked.

6 Season well.

Italian beef with dried plums

Dried plums (or prunes) make a very positive contribution to stews as they thicken, sweeten and darken the sauces naturally. The Belgians, for example, have a traditional rabbit and prune dish, and in Poland you will find recipes that combine prunes with venison or lamb.

This Italian recipe is an unusual one – the most important ingredient is the vinegar, as it prevents the sauce from becoming over-sweet.

Serves 4

510g (1lb 2oz) brisket/silverside, sliced thickly

1 onion, sliced

450g (1lb) carrots, chopped

2 garlic cloves, chopped

3 cloves

2 tbsp olive oil

1/4 tsp nutmeg

1/4 glass sweet wine / sherry

1/2 glass red wine vinegar

570ml (20fl oz / 1 pint) tomato sauce (see page 227)

6-8 prunes / dried plums, chopped (see page 220)

To season: Salt and pepper

Optional:
2-3 rashers bacon, chopped

To serve: Parmesan shavings

1 Brown the beef on both sides in olive oil.

2 Add the onion, bacon (if using), carrots, cloves, nutmeg, garlic, vinegar and wine and cook for 5-10 minutes.

3 Add the tomato sauce and plums. Simmer gently for 2 hours.

4 Season well and add extra vinegar if the stew is not quite sharp enough.

5 Slice the meat and serve sprinkled with Parmesan cheese.

Pork à la Normande

Don't use cooking apples for this recipe, as the slices will turn into a thick purée.

Serves 2

2 pork chops

30g (1oz) butter

1 onion, chopped

1 garlic clove, chopped

1 eating apple, peeled, sliced

2 tbsp brandy/Calvados

225ml (8fl oz) cider

55ml (2fl oz) single cream

Optional:
Herbs e.g. thyme or sage

To season: Salt and pepper

1 Brown the pork gently in the butter.

2 Add the onion and garlic to the pan and cook for a few minutes.

3 Add the apple slices and brown. Either remove these and return them to the pan at the end or leave them during the cooking.

4 Stir in the brandy and ignite.

5 When the flames have died down, pour in the cider, season well, add any herbs and simmer for 20-30 minutes until the pork is fully cooked.

6 Remove the pork and keep warm.

7 Stir the cream into the juices in the pan, replace any apple slices and warm through. Check the seasoning and either serve the sauce separately or pour it over the chops just before serving.

Baked pork and pears

Instead of grilling the meat, you can use cheaper cuts and cook them slowly in the oven.

Serves 2

2 spare rib chops

2 firm pears, peeled, halved

2-3 potatoes, sliced

Sage, crumbled

Brown sugar

Olive oil

To season: Salt and pepper

1 Arrange the sliced potatoes in a layer in an oiled baking tin.

2 Arrange the meat and sage over the potatoes and season well.

3 Arrange the pears, cut-side down, on top of the meat.

4 Drizzle over extra oil and bake at 180°C (360°F / Gas Mark 4) for about 20 minutes.

5 Remove the tin from the oven, turn over the meat and replace the pear halves, cut-side up, on top.

6 Sprinkle several tablespoons of brown sugar over the pears.

7 Continue baking for about 30-40 minutes until the meat and potatoes are cooked and the sugar has caramelised.

Pears, pork and blue cheese

Serves 2

2 pork chops / steaks

Olive oil

1 red onion, sliced

2-3 pears, peeled

Rosemary

55g (2oz) blue cheese, cubed

To season: Salt and pepper

1. Season the pork and grill on a medium heat for 20-30 minutes, turning occasionally.
2. In the meantime, heat oil in a frying pan and gently fry the onion, pears, rosemary and seasoning for 5-10 minutes.
3. Add the pork to the pear mixture and scatter with extra rosemary and blue cheese.
4. Heat the pan under the grill until the cheese starts to melt.

Chicken and spinach yoghurt curry

Serves 2

2-3 chicken breasts

225g (8oz) spinach, chopped

1 onion, chopped

1 garlic clove, crushed

1 tbsp vegetable oil

1 tsp cumin, ground

1 tsp chilli powder / chillies, crushed

1 tsp turmeric powder

1/2 tsp ginger, ground/crushed

225ml (8fl oz) plain yoghurt

Oil for frying

To season: Salt and pepper

To garnish:
Coriander, fresh, chopped / Cardamom, whole

To serve: Rice / naan bread

1. Mix the spices, yoghurt and 1 tbsp of oil together in a bowl and marinate the chicken pieces for 1-3 hours.
2. Heat some oil in a pan and gently fry the onion and garlic until transparent.
3. Add the chicken pieces, lifted out of the marinade with a fork, and simmer for 5 minutes.
4. Scrape in the yoghurt marinade and add together with the spinach, salt and about 140ml (5fl oz / 1/4 pint) water.
5. Bring to the boil and then simmer for 30-40 minutes until the chicken is well cooked.
6. Stir occasionally and, if necessary, add more water so there will be a good amount of sauce, but don't let it become too thin and watery.
7. Adjust the seasoning to taste, garnish and serve with rice or naan bread.

Shepherd's pie with carrots

Serves 4

450g (1lb) minced lamb

450g (1lb) potatoes

1 onion, chopped

2-3 carrots, peeled and chopped

55g (2oz) peas

1 tbsp tomato purée

1/2 glass red wine and/or stock

1 tsp Worcester sauce

1 bay leaf

1 tbsp thyme

Oil

Milk

Butter

To season: Salt and pepper

Optional: Cheese, grated

1   Fry the onion for a few minutes in the oil, then add the mince and brown.

2   Add the vegetables and fry for a few more minutes.

3   Add the tomato purée, wine/stock, Worcester sauce and herbs and cook for about 20 minutes.

4   Meanwhile, boil the potatoes and then mash with milk, butter and seasoning.

5   Spoon the mince mixture into a large casserole dish and spread a layer of mashed potato over the top.

6   Sprinkle cheese on top, if you like, then bake at 190°C (380°F / Gas Mark 5) for about 30 minutes until brown and bubbling.

Corned beef and beetroot hash

This dish is equally delicious if made with carrots instead of beetroot.

Serves 2-3

1 tin (340g/12oz) corned beef, diced

450g (1lb) beetroot, peeled and diced

2 medium potatoes, diced

1 onion, chopped

Oil

To season: Salt and pepper

1   Fry the onion gently in the oil until soft.

2   Add the potatoes to the pan with the corned beef and beetroot.

3   Season and cook gently, stirring regularly, until the potatoes are almost cooked.

4   Squash down the mixture to form a more solid mass and leave to cook until the bottom becomes brown and crispy.

5   Brown the top under the grill.

Chicken and cucumber

Serves 2

2 chicken pieces

1/2 cucumber, peeled, cubed

1/4 glass sherry

285ml (10fl oz / 1/2 pint) stock

1 tbsp flour

85ml (3fl oz) soured cream

Olive oil

To season: Salt and pepper

To garnish: Cucumber, sliced

1. Fry the chicken pieces in the oil until brown and then stir in the flour.

2. Add the sherry and stock, heat until the sauce thickens and then cook for 30 minutes. Add further stock to prevent the chicken from drying out.

3. Add the cubed cucumber, season well and continue to cook for a further 10 minutes.

4. Stir in soured cream and garnish with cucumber.

Fish

Fish goes surprisingly well with tomatoes and, even more unusually, with summer fruit!

Baked fish, pesto and tomatoes

Serves 2-3

450g (1lb) white fish e.g. cod, skin removed

4-6 cherry tomatoes, or medium-sized tomato quarters

Mayonnaise

Pesto

2-3 slices bread, crumbled

Parsley, chopped

Lemon juice

Oil

To season: Salt and pepper

1. Place the fish in an oiled baking tin.

2. Season with salt and pepper.

3. Surround with the tomatoes.

4. Spread the fish with a layer of mayonnaise mixed with pesto.

5. Mix the breadcrumbs with the parsley and scatter over the whole dish.

6. Sprinkle over lemon juice.

7. Bake at 190°C (380°F / Gas Mark 5) for 15 minutes or until the fish is white and flakes easily and the topping is crisp and brown.

Salmon, cucumber and strawberries

Serves 2

2 salmon fillets

Salsa:

1 cucumber, diced

1 red pepper / yellow pepper, diced

1/2 onion, diced

1 tbsp fresh coriander/parsley, finely chopped

4 tbsp wine vinegar

115g (4oz) strawberries, hulled, diced

Sauce:

30g (1oz) butter

1 tsp garlic, finely chopped

1 tbsp honey

1 tbsp tomato ketchup

1 tbsp lemon juice

1   Mix together the cucumber, pepper, onion, herbs and vinegar in a bowl. Cover and chill for at least 1 hour.

2   Melt the butter and gently fry the garlic. Stir in the honey, ketchup and lemon juice and cook for 2-3 minutes. Use this sauce to coat the fish.

3   When ready to cook the fish, brush the sauce on the salmon pieces and grill for 4-5 minutes on each side.

4   Serve topped with the cucumber mixture, to which you have added the strawberries.

A summery combination of salmon and strawberries.

Chapter 6
Desserts

EVERYDAY PUDDINGS

BAKED FRUIT

STEWED FRUIT

PANCAKES

PIES, FLANS AND TARTS

FRUIT IN BATTER

FOOLS

VEGETABLE DESSERTS

ICE CREAMS AND SORBETS

Ice creams

Sweet sorbets

Savoury sorbets

EVERYDAY PUDDINGS

For most fruit puddings, any mixture of fruit is acceptable. Even strawberries, not usually cooked, can make a welcome addition to a summer berry crumble or mixed fruit sponge.

When using fruit such as gooseberries or rhubarb, you will need extra sugar, but as sweetness is a matter of taste, the quantities in the recipes are really only a suggestion. If you need to add extra sugar after fruit has been stewed or puréed, use icing or caster sugar as granulated sugar will need to be dissolved first. You can also add variety to any fruit mix by including your favourite flavourings – in solid or essence form – such as ginger, vanilla or almond, or by stirring in extra items such as chopped crystallised fruit, chocolate, marmalade or mincemeat.

Remember to remove all plum or damson stones before cooking.

Spotted Dick

This is really a sponge with raisins, but I always add grated fruit or fruit pieces for a moister pudding. This version uses cooking apple, but you can use pears instead.

Serves 4

115g (4oz) butter

115g (4oz) sugar

2 medium eggs, beaten

Half a medium cooking apple, peeled and diced / grated

55g (2oz) raisins

115g (4oz) self-raising flour

Optional:
15g (1/2 oz) ground almonds to replace 15g of flour

1   Cream the butter and sugar.

2   Stir in the beaten eggs.

3   Stir in the fruit.

4   Fold in the flour and ground almonds, if including these.

5   Bake at 180°C (360°F / Gas Mark 4) for 40-45 minutes.

6   Make sure you test the sponge mixture and not a piece of fruit when checking if it is properly cooked.

Fruit crumble

Serves 4

Roughly 450g (1lb) any fruit, e.g. apples, rhubarb, plums, damsons, gooseberries, blackberries, black-currants, etc.

115g (4oz) plain flour

55g (2oz) butter

85g (3oz) sugar

Extra sugar for fruit

1 Rub the butter into the flour until it forms crumbs.

2 Stir in the sugar.

3 Cut up the fruit and use to half- or three-quarters-fill a pie dish. Sprinkle on extra sugar if the fruit needs it.

4 Spoon the crumble mixture over the fruit. Don't press down if you want a crumbly topping.

5 Bake at 180°C (360°F / Gas Mark 4) for 35 minutes.

＊ For healthier crumbles, replace 15-30g (0.5-1oz) plain flour with an equal weight of porridge oats and add some chopped nuts.

Most fruit mixes will work well in a crumble.

Pear, chocolate and nut pudding

Serves 4

115g (4oz) blanched almonds / hazelnuts, chopped

140g (5oz) self-raising flour

170g (6oz) butter

140g (5oz) light brown sugar

2 eggs, beaten

5 small, ripe pears, peeled

55g (2oz) dark chocolate, chopped

1 Mix together the nuts, flour and butter to form a crumbly mixture.

2 Stir in the sugar and eggs.

3 Chop up two pears and add with the chocolate pieces.

4 Spoon this mixture into a greased baking tin or oven dish.

5 Slice the remaining pears and arrange the slices over the pudding mixture.

6 Press the fruit down lightly into the mixture and bake at 170°C (340°F / Gas Mark 3) for about 45 minutes until cooked through. Serve warm or cold.

Fruit sponge

If the fruit in this dish is apple, you may know this recipe as Eve's pudding. I never add sugar to cooking apples as they always seem sweet enough – simply peel, chop and fill the dish with the fruit before spooning on the sponge topping.

(For richer, heavier sponges replace 15g [0.5oz] flour with ground almonds.)

Serves 4

450g (1lb) any fruit or fruit mix, e.g. cooking apples, rhubarb, redcurrants and raspberries

115g (4oz) butter

115g (4oz) sugar

2 medium eggs, beaten

115g (4oz) self-raising flour

Optional:
1/2 tsp vanilla essence / ground cinnamon

1 Half- or three-quarter-fill a pie dish with fruit and sprinkle on sugar if required.

2 Cream the butter and sugar.

3 Stir in the beaten eggs and add essence, if using.

4 Fold in the flour and any ground spices.

5 Spoon the mixture over the fruit.

6 Bake at 180°C (360°F / Gas Mark 4) for 40-45 minutes.

✳ To test if a sponge is cooked properly, insert a skewer or knife. It should come out cleanly with no mixture sticking to it.

Summer (or autumn) pudding

The well-known summer pudding uses fruits such as blackcurrants, redcurrants, strawberries and raspberries, but you can also make this pudding using autumn fruits such as plums, rhubarb, blackberries, gooseberries, pears or cooking apples.

As you need to chill the pudding for several hours, it is a good idea to make it the day before it is needed.

Serves 4

450g (1lb) mixed fruit

3-4 slices day-old bread, crustless, cut into strips

55-115g (2-4oz) sugar (depending on the fruit)

1   Pre-cook the fruit. For berries and currants, simply stew or microwave gently with some sugar until the juices start to flow, but stop cooking before they stew down completely. For autumn fruits, stew them gently in a little water and sugar until they are completely cooked, adding extra water or apple juice to make sure they produce a good quantity of juice.

2   Line the base and sides of a dish completely with bread. If you dip each strip in the fruit juices first you won't get bald, white patches on the bread.

3   Using a slotted spoon, fill the bread-lined dish with fruit and then add some of the juice.

4   Use bread to form a top and try to fill all the gaps.

5   Spoon over enough of the juice to darken all the bread, retaining the rest for use when serving the dish.

6   Cover the pudding with a saucer that fits inside the edges of the dish and keep this pressed down by placing a heavy object such as a tin on top.

7   Chill overnight in the fridge.

8   When serving, turn out the pudding (or serve from the dish) and pour more juice over any white bread that is showing. Hand round the rest as a sauce.

Summer pudding is great with cream, yoghurt or ice cream.

Meringue

If you have some egg whites left over, perhaps after making ice cream, it is very easy to make your own meringues. Although all the recipes you come across will stress that you must use caster sugar, I have made excellent meringues using a mixture of granulated and icing sugar.

Egg whites

55g (2oz) caster sugar / half-granulated, half-icing sugar for each egg white

Whisk the egg whites in a bowl until stiff and then gradually add in the sugar a little at a time, whisking until the mixture is stiff and shiny.

Spoon out dollops on to a well-greased baking sheet, spaced so they don't touch each other.

Bake for 1 hour in a cool oven e.g. 140°C (280°F / Gas Mark 1).

Turn off the oven and leave the meringues inside to cool completely.

Eton mess

This is a very English pudding made by mixing summer fruit such as strawberries or raspberries with meringue, sugar and whipped cream. It does indeed look a bit of a mess – but tastes delicious.

Serves 2-3

450g (1lb) strawberries/ raspberries, hulled

1 tbsp icing sugar

570ml (20fl oz / 1 pint) whipping cream (or half cream, half yoghurt)

6 meringue shells

1   Mix together half the fruit with the sugar and purée in a blender or mash with a fork.

2   If using strawberries, chop the rest into large pieces. Reserve several pieces of fruit for decoration.

3   Whip the cream to form soft peaks.

4   Chill everything until you are ready to serve.

5   Stir the whole berries or fruit pieces into the cream.

6   Break up the meringue into small pieces and stir into the cream mixture together with any yoghurt.

7   Stir through the fruit purée for a marbled effect.

8   Decorate with a few choice pieces of fruit.

Toffee apples

Serves 4

4 eating apples, well washed

4 wooden sticks

225g (8oz) sugar, e.g. demerara or brown

100ml (3 1/2 fl oz) water

1 tsp white wine vinegar

2 tbsp golden syrup

30g (1oz) butter

Optional:
Nuts, finely chopped

1 Push the sticks into the stalk end of the apples until the apples are held firmly.

2 Cover a tray in lightly greased aluminium foil or non-stick baking paper.

3 Heat the sugar and water.

4 Add the rest of the ingredients and bring to the boil.

5 Boil for 8-10 minutes until the temperature has reached 140°C (280°F / Gas Mark 1). If you don't have a sugar thermometer, test that the toffee is ready by dropping a little into very cold water. It should form a hard ball that breaks when you snap it, rather than staying stretchy. You should also find that the toffee consistency in the pan will have changed.

6 Turn off the heat and then quickly rotate each apple in the toffee before standing it on the foil to set.

7 For a variation, stir chopped nuts into the toffee before coating the apples.

Apple snow

Serves 2-3

Note: this recipe contains raw egg

450g (1lb) cooking apples, cored, peeled

2 tbsp sugar

2 eggs, separated

140ml (5fl oz / 1/4 pint) double cream

Optional:
Lemon zest

1 Cook the apples with the sugar and lemon zest (if using) to form a thick purée.

2 Cool the mixture and then stir in the egg yolks.

3 Whisk the egg whites and cream separately and then either fold both into the apple mixture or just use the egg white and reserve the cream as a topping.

4 Chill for 30 minutes before serving.

BAKED FRUIT

Whether simple or more complex dishes, baking fruit in the oven provides wonderfully hot puddings that go well with custard, cream or ice cream.

Baked pears and plums

Unless using small plums, these fruit are usually halved or cut into slices before being baked with sugar and spices. You could also stand peeled pears on bases that have been cut flat to bake them whole.

Serves 2-3

2-3 pears or 3-6 plums

Brown sugar

Spices, e.g. nutmeg, cinnamon, cloves

Optional:
Sweet wine

1   Peel, core and halve/slice 2 or 3 large pears, or pit and halve several plums.

2   Place cut-side up in a greased baking dish.

3   Scatter over a mixture of brown sugar and spices such as nutmeg or cinnamon and a couple of whole cloves. If you want to produce lots of extra juice, pour a little sweet wine or water into the dish.

4   Bake for about 30 minutes in a hot oven – 190°C (380°F / Gas Mark 5) – until the juices have started to caramelise.

Hot, spicy baked plums are the perfect autumnal sweet.

Toasted breadcrumbs work well with any fruit purée.

Danish fruit dessert

Although commonly made with apple purée, this dessert is perfect with other fruit such as plums, raspberries or redcurrants.

Serves 3-4

225g (8oz) fruit, e.g. redcurrants

225g (8oz) or 6-8 slices of bread as fine breadcrumbs

85g (3oz) butter

4-6 tbsp brown sugar

To serve:
Whipped cream

1 Melt the butter with 2 tbsp sugar and gently fry the breadcrumbs.

2 Place half the crumbs in the base of a greased baking dish.

3 Top with the fruit mixed with the rest of the sugar. (Or you could replace this with any puréed, sweetened fruit.)

4 Finish with the other half of the crumbs.

5 Bake at 180°C (360°F / Gas Mark 4) for 25 minutes.

6 Serve warm with whipped cream.

Baked apples

Still a great pudding, this has rather gone out of favour in recent years but is definitely worth reintroducing.

1 apple per person

Mincemeat or dried fruit and honey / brown sugar

To serve:
Cream / yoghurt / ice cream / custard

1   Choose one large apple for each person – both cooking and eating varieties will work but cooking apples will go particularly soft inside.

2   Core and place on a baking sheet. There is no need to peel but, if you don't want them to burst, cut a ring around each apple across its diameter to let out the steam.

3   Fill the centre with a mixture of mincemeat or dried fruit and honey or brown sugar.

4   Bake at 180°C (360°F / Gas Mark 4) for about 25 minutes.

5   Leave to cool as they will be very hot.

6   Serve with cream, yoghurt, ice cream or custard.

Fruity bread pudding

You can use any fruit for this dessert, including pears, plums or raspberries, fresh or dried. Change the flavourings if you prefer mixed spice, almond or ginger to vanilla or cinnamon.

Serves 4

4-6 slices (225g [8oz]) bread, torn into small pieces

115-170g (4-6oz) fruit, chopped

55g (2oz) raisins

285ml (10fl oz / 1/2 pint) milk

100g (3 1/2 oz) brown sugar

55g (2oz) butter

1 egg

1 tsp vanilla

2 tsp spices, e.g. cinnamon/ nutmeg, ground

1   Mix the bread, cinnamon, chopped fruit and raisins in a bowl.

2   If you have time, pour over the milk and leave to soak into the bread for 20-40 minutes.

3   Heat the milk (if not used yet), sugar and butter gently until the butter melts.

4   Whisk the egg with vanilla in a bowl and stir in the buttery mixture.

5   Pour this mixture over the bread.

6   Stir well to break up any lumps and then transfer to a greased oven dish or baking tin.

7   Set in a larger tin half-filled with hot water and bake at 180°C (360°F / Gas Mark 4) for about 1-1 1/4 hours. Test that a knife blade inserted in the centre comes out cleanly.

STEWED FRUIT

Poaching or stewing is a good cooking method if you are using up the end of a glut and have dry, tough or sour fruit as it will always produce soft, tender pieces. All you need is water (or wine), sugar and flavourings such as cinnamon, vanilla or nutmeg. Stewed fruit dishes are often described as compotes.

Poached pears

Serves 4

2-3 pears, peeled

485ml (17fl oz) red wine

255g (9oz) sugar

2-3 whole cloves

Cinnamon stick

1 Bring the wine and spices to the boil in a large saucepan and then simmer for a few minutes.

2 Add the sugar and cook until dissolved.

3 Either leave the pears whole but with stalk intact or cut vertically in half or quarters and remove the cores.

4 Place the pears in the pan, cover and simmer for about 40-50 minutes until well cooked. If lying on their sides, turn halfway through the cooking to give an even colour.

5 Remove the pears with a slotted spoon and place in a serving dish.

6 Strain the liquid, return to the pan and boil until reduced to a thick syrup. Pour over the fruit and either serve warm or chill for several hours.

Poires Belle Hélène

Poached pears – 1 per person (see above)

Chocolate sauce:
55g (2oz) plain chocolate

1-2 tbsp milk or cream

To serve:
Whipped cream / ice cream

1 Poach the pears as for poached pears (see above) but use water rather than red wine for the syrup and flavour with either cinnamon or vanilla. If you want the pears cold, chill them until ready to serve.

2 Make a chocolate sauce by melting dark chocolate pieces in the microwave or over hot water with a little milk and then quickly stir in enough cream or more milk to give a pouring consistency.

3 Place a pear on each plate, pour over the chocolate sauce and serve with ice cream or whipped cream.

Dried fruit compote

Having dried some of your fruits in the autumn, you can use them to create a simple winter pudding that makes the most of their lovely flavours and colours. Just poach the fruit with spices and serve with cream or yoghurt.

You could add nuts or seeds to this pudding for extra wholesomeness.

Serves 4

510g (1lb 2oz) dried, mixed fruit, e.g. apples, plums, pears, raisins and apricots, whole/chopped

200ml (7fl oz) orange juice

Spices, e.g. broken cinnamon stick, whole cloves

Optional: Honey/sugar; Nuts/seeds

To serve:
Cream / yoghurt

1. Soak the fruit in water overnight.
2. Strain the fruit and then poach in the orange juice with the spices for 10-15 minutes, or cook in a microwave for 5 minutes.
3. If needed, add 1 tbsp of honey or sugar and stir in any nuts or seeds.
4. Remove the spices and leave to cool.

PANCAKES

Any cooked fruit can be used to fill a pancake or the thinner crêpe, and dishes can range from the very simple to sophisticated alcohol and cream concoctions. As an alternative, you can cook fruit together with batter on top of the hob to make a sweet pancake-style dish known as a tansy. This works particularly well with fruit such as gooseberries, apples, plums, pears or damsons.

Fruit pancakes

Serves 4

115g (4oz) plain flour

Pinch of salt

1 large egg

140-200ml (5-7fl oz) milk

Berries / fruit purée

Optional:
1 tbsp melted butter

To serve:
Sugar / cream / maple syrup

1. Sift the flour into a bowl and add the salt.
2. Make a well in the centre, stir in the egg and then beat in enough milk for a pouring batter.
3. Just before cooking, you can stir in melted butter for a richer version.
4. Make pancakes in the normal way and keep warm if making several.
5. Fill with warm fruit purée such as apples, pears or mixed berries that have been gently stewed with sugar.
6. Serve sprinkled with sugar/cream/syrup.

Jamaican pancakes

Although this dish originated in a restaurant where the pancakes were served with bananas and rum, in our family we have adapted it to suit any fruit we happen to have to hand.

1 pancake/crêpe per person

Berries / sweetened fruit purée

Liqueur (e.g. your own home-made fruit liqueur, Chambord if using raspberries, or brandy if using plums)

Chocolate, plain, broken into pieces

Milk

Icing sugar

To serve:
Ice cream / whipped cream

1. Place a pancake on a plate and spoon on some fruit purée. If using fresh fruit, you may want to sprinkle this with a little sugar.
2. Add 1 capful of liqueur.
3. Fold over the pancake 'corners' to make a parcel and heat in a microwave for a minute.
4. Make a sauce by melting the chocolate in a bowl with a little milk and then stirring in enough extra milk to give a pouring consistency.
5. Sprinkle icing sugar on the pancake, drizzle over some chocolate sauce and serve immediately with ice cream / whipped cream.

Damson tansy

Serves 4

2 eating apples, peeled, cored, sliced

200g (7oz) damsons, stoned, chopped

1 tbsp butter

40-55g (1 1/2 -2oz) brown sugar

4 eggs, separated

3 tbsp sour cream / yoghurt / crème fraiche

1/2 tsp cloves, ground

1/2 tsp cinnamon, ground

1   Melt the butter in a pan and gently cook the fruit and half the sugar until soft.

2   Stir in the spices and remove from the heat. Leave to cool.

3   Beat the egg yolks with the sour cream, yoghurt or crème fraiche and stir into the fruit.

4   Whisk the egg whites until stiff and fold into the mixture with a metal spoon.

5   Return to a low heat and cook without stirring until the mixture has set.

6   Sprinkle the remaining sugar over the top and brown for a few minutes under a hot grill to caramelise the sugar.

7   Serve straight away.

PIES, FLANS AND TARTS

When making pies, flans and tarts there are a number of different ways to arrange pastry and fruit:

- Cover the fruit and create a pie with a pastry top only.
- Make a Tarte Tatin by turning the tart out on to a plate and on to its crust so that the fruit layer is now on top.
- Use the pastry for both base and top.
- Make an open tart by pre-baking the pastry and then adding fresh or pre-cooked fruit plus filling.
- Form the top as an open lattice.
- Make individual fruit tarts.
- Fold over the pastry into a turnover.

The normal pastry used for fruit pies is shortcrust (see page 90), rich shortcrust that incorporates eggs, or sweet shortcrust that includes additional sugar (see overleaf for these). However, you could also use bought puff pastry or even sheets of filo pastry.

Rich (or sweet) shortcrust pastry

This recipe makes roughly the amount of pastry needed for most of the pastry recipes in this book.

340g (12oz) plain flour

Pinch of salt

170-200g (6-7oz) cold butter, cut into pieces

2 eggs, beaten (or use just the yolks for even richer pastry)

1-2 tbsp cold water / milk

Optional:
40g (1 1/2 oz) icing sugar – for sweet pastry

1 Sift the flour (and sugar if included) into a bowl and stir in the salt.

2 Use a knife or your fingers to lightly mix the butter into the dry ingredients to form a crumbly mixture.

3 Add the eggs and a little water or milk and form into a soft dough.

4 Chill in the fridge before using.

To cook a pie with only a top:

1 Fill the pie dish two-thirds with fruit and add sugar if required.

2 Roll out the pastry 1.5cm (1/2") larger than the rim of the pie dish.

3 Cut round the outer edge of the pastry to form a strip.

4 Wet the pie dish rim and stick on the pastry all the way round.

5 Wet the surface of the pastry rim. Lay the rest of the pastry on top and seal the joint by pressing along the rim with a fork.

6 Make slits in the pastry top to let out steam.

7 Bake at 180°C (360°F / Gas Mark 4) for 30-40 minutes.

Redcurrant and blackcurrant pie

Serves 4

225g (8oz) fruit, mixed

Shortcrust pastry (see page 90) or rich shortcrust pastry / sweet shortcrust pastry made with 340g (12oz) flour (see above)

Sugar

To glaze:
Beaten egg / milk

1 Line a prepared pie dish with pastry.

2 Fill the dish with the mixed fruit.

3 Scatter over a good few tablespoons of sugar.

4 Cover with a pie crust. Press the edges to seal and cut a few slits in the top.

5 Dust with sugar or brush with beaten egg or milk.

6 Bake at 180°C (360°F / Gas Mark 4) for 30-40 minutes.

7 This pie is delicious served either hot or cold.

Rhubarb and almond tart

This is a very simple recipe that would work equally well with any other fruit, such as plums or pears, that goes well with almonds.

Serves 4

900g (2lb) rhubarb, chopped

540g (1lb 3oz) sugar

115g (4oz) butter

3 eggs

2 tbsp white wine

255g (9oz) plain flour

2 tsp baking powder

140ml (5fl oz / 1/4 pint) sour cream / yoghurt

1 tsp cinnamon

55g (2oz) ground almonds

Optional:
Almond essence

To serve:
Icing sugar

1 Place the rhubarb in a bowl, sprinkle on 400g (14oz) sugar, cover and stand for 1-2 hours. (To make sure that the rhubarb cooks properly later in the oven, heat the bowl in a microwave for 3-4 minutes or use fruit that has been previously frozen so that the cell walls have started to break down.)

2 Cream the butter with 85g (3oz) of the sugar.

3 Beat 1 egg and add with the wine to the creamed butter.

4 Sift the flour and baking powder and fold in.

5 Lightly knead the mixture and then wrap the dough in cling film and chill for about 30 minutes.

6 Use the dough to line a greased 25cm (10") flan tin.

7 Strain the rhubarb and arrange over the pastry. Bake for 25 minutes at 180°C (360°F / Gas Mark 4).

8 Beat together the cream/yoghurt, remaining eggs and sugar. Stir in the cinnamon and ground almonds and mix well. You could also add a drop or two of almond essence.

9 Take the tart out of the oven, pour over the almond cream and return to the oven to bake for another 20-25 minutes.

10 Serve sprinkled with icing sugar.

✻ Freezing rhubarb first will make it quicker to cook.

Plum Tarte Tatin

This recipe is made in a series of steps:
- Prepare a circle of pastry.
- Make caramel syrup with butter, water and sugar.
  This will go in the bottom of the cake tin or pan.
- Add the fruit.
- Top with the pastry circle.
- Bake for the required amount of time in the oven.
- Turn out the tart like a cake, so the fruit and syrup are now on the top.

Serves 4

200g (7oz) ready-made puff pastry (or use sweet shortcrust)

6-10 large plums, stoned and halved

30ml (1fl oz) water

100g (3 1/2 oz) brown sugar

30g (1oz) butter

Optional:
1/2 tsp cinnamon

Substitute the plums with damsons

You will also need:
Ovenproof pan that can go on the hob, or separate cake tin

1   In a pan, dissolve the sugar in the water and then add the butter and cinnamon (if using) and cook for a few minutes.

2   If using the same pan, arrange the plums carefully over the top of the syrup (cut-side down) packing them together firmly. Simmer on a low heat until the sugar and butter caramelise and the plums have cooked.

3   If using a cake tin, pour in the syrup and arrange the fruit on top. Bake the fruit in the oven at 190°C (380°F / Gas Mark 5) for about 20 minutes.

4   Roll out the pastry, prick gently with a fork, and then press it over the plums, tucking in the edges.

5   Put the pan in an oven preheated to 190°C (380°F / Gas Mark 5) and cook for about 35-40 minutes, until the pastry has risen and is golden brown.

6   Remove the pan from the oven and leave to cool for about 1 hour.

7   Run a knife round the edge of the tart and turn it out on to a plate held firmly over the pan. You may need to lift out any plums that stick.

Pear and blackberry flan

Serves 4

450g (1lb) pears, peeled, cored

170g (6oz) blackberries

170g (6oz) plain flour

30g (1oz) icing sugar

85g (3oz) butter

Filling:

1 egg

85g (3oz) sugar

1 tbsp plain flour

Grated rind and juice of 1 orange

1 Make the pastry by mixing the flour, icing sugar and butter to form a crumbly mixture. If needed, add a little cold water so you can form a soft dough.

2 Chill for half an hour and then use it to line a greased flan tin.

3 For a crisper base, bake blind for 10 minutes (see page 91).

4 Slice the pears and arrange a layer over the pastry shell.

5 Sprinkle over the blackberries.

6 Make the filling by beating the egg with the sugar and then stirring in the orange juice and rind. Fold in the flour and spoon the mixture over the fruit.

7 Bake at 200°C (400°F / Gas Mark 6) for about 40 minutes until the filling is firm.

Strawberry flan

Serves 4

Sweet shortcrust pastry using 225g (8oz) flour

450g (1lb) strawberries

30g (1oz) plain flour

310ml (11fl oz) milk

30g (1oz) caster sugar

2 egg yolks

2-3 tbsp red seedless jam

1 Line a flan tin with pastry and bake blind for 15 minutes at 200°C (400°F / Gas Mark 6) (see page 91).

2 Leave the pastry to cool.

3 Make a custard by blending the flour and sugar with the milk and then whisking in the egg yolks.

4 Set the bowl over a pan of hot water and heat the mixture gently, continuing to whisk until the custard thickens.

5 Leave it to cool.

6 Pour the custard into the cold pastry shell.

7 Halve the fruit and arrange in circles on the custard.

8 Warm the jam with 1 tbsp water and use it as a fruit glaze.

9 Chill before serving.

Cheesecake with apple

As well as using pastry, you can create sweet flans with a biscuit base. This is made by crushing biscuits such as digestives or gingernuts and mixing them with a little melted butter.

Serves 4

115g (4oz) digestive biscuits, crushed

55g (2oz) butter

85-115g (3-4oz) apple purée

340g (12oz) curd / cream cheese

85g (3oz) sugar

85ml (3fl oz) double cream

2 eggs

1/2 tsp lemon juice

85g (3oz) sultanas

1 Melt the butter, mix with the biscuit crumbs and press into the base of a flan tin. Chill while you prepare the rest of the ingredients.

2 Beat the eggs and sugar together and then stir in the curd or cream cheese, lemon juice and cream. Beat again and then add the sultanas.

3 Spoon a thick, even layer of apple purée over the biscuit base and then fill the tin with the cheese mixture.

4 Bake at 180°C (360°F / Gas Mark 4) for about 30 minutes and then turn off the oven and leave the tin to cool completely.

Other ways to combine cheesecake and fruit:
* Use different fruit purées such as pear, blackcurrant or raspberry spread over the biscuit base.
* Spread fruit purée over the cooked cheesecake as a topping.
* Top the cooked cheesecake with chopped or whole fresh fruit such as strawberries, raspberries or blackberries.

FRUIT IN BATTER

Pieces of fruit can either be dipped in batter, fried and served sprinkled with sugar, or you can bake batter and fruit together as a pudding. When making fritters, the fruit must be dry and the batter thick enough to coat the pieces. You will then have juicy fruit inside a crisp, crunchy coating.

Apple fritters

Either use the fritter batter recipe on page 80, or try this one using cider for a stronger apple flavour.

Serves 2-3

2 eating apples, peeled

140g (5oz) plain flour

1 egg, separated

255ml (9fl oz) cider

Pinch salt

Oil for frying

To serve:
Icing sugar

Hot fruit coulis / sugar syrup

1 Core the apples, cut off the top and bottom and then slice thickly (1cm [3/8"] slices). If they will be left for any length of time, turn them in lemon juice.

2 Make the batter by stirring the egg yolk into the flour and salt and slowly beating in enough cider for a good coating consistency.

3 Pour 2cm (3/4") oil in a pan and heat for frying.

4 When ready to serve, whisk the egg white and fold into the batter. Dry the fruit slices and dip into the batter until completely coated. Add them to the oil a few at a time.

5 Fry for about 3 minutes, until golden brown, and then drain on kitchen paper.

6 Serve sprinkled with icing sugar, with a hot fruit coulis (see page 231) or make a sugar syrup by dissolving sugar in cider and then boiling this down to a thick sauce.

Chinese toffee apples

These are wedges of apple in batter, coated in a sugary toffee glaze.

Serves 2-3

2 eating apples, peeled and cut into 6-8 sections

lemon juice

55g (2oz) plain flour

1 egg

1 tsp sesame oil

Peanut oil for frying

170g (6oz) sugar

2 tbsp sesame seeds

1 Prepare the apples and keep in water with added lemon juice.

2 Mix the egg, flour, and sesame oil together and add enough water to make a batter that has the consistency of double cream.

3 Dry the apples and dip into the batter. Deep-fry a few at a time for about 3 minutes until golden brown. Drain well on kitchen paper.

4 In a separate pan, mix the sugar and seeds with 2 tbsp of the frying oil and heat gently until it starts to caramelise.

5 Hold the apple pieces on toothpicks and dip them into this toffee, then plunge them into ice-cold water to set.

Plum clafoutis

The classic French recipe uses fresh cherries, which stay discrete during baking, but it would work just as well with raspberries or blackberries. When using large fruits like plums you may need to cook them first or you will over-bake the batter before the fruit is soft enough to eat. This means that the result will be more like a 'jam and batter' pudding, but it still tastes delicious and is quite different from more familiar crumbles, pies and sponges.

Richer versions of this recipe suggest either adding alcohol to the batter or first marinating the fruit for several hours in alcohol and sugar. This not only improves the flavour but will also soften the fruit. For a special dessert, marinate plums using a suitable alcohol such as brandy and omit the first stage of cooking.

Serves 4

340g (12oz) plums, halved, stoned

2 tbsp butter

2 tbsp sugar

Optional:
1 tsp vanilla essence

Batter:
2 eggs

2 tbsp sugar

100g (3 1/2 oz) plain flour

140-285ml (5-10fl oz / 1/4 - 1/2 pint) milk, or use a mixture of milk and cream

To serve: Icing sugar / caster sugar

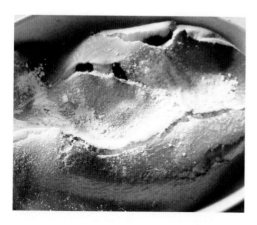

1 Heat the butter in a pan, add the plums, sugar and vanilla essence (if using) and cook gently for 5-10 minutes.

2 Transfer the cooked (or marinated) fruit to a greased baking tin and heat in the oven while you make the batter.

3 Beat the sugar and eggs together and then blend with the flour. Stir in enough milk so that the mixture is smooth and creamy.

4 Pour the batter over the fruit in the hot tin and bake for about 30-40 minutes at 190°C (380°F / Gas Mark 5) until the pudding is completely cooked and the batter golden and well risen.

5 Serve warm, sprinkled with a little icing or caster sugar.

FOOLS

Fools are rich, creamy puddings that combine stewed or puréed fruit with whipped cream and a range of other dairy products such as mascarpone cheese, yoghurt, fromage frais or even custard. They work particularly well with sourer fruits such as rhubarb and gooseberry, but any strongly flavoured fruit would make a good fool. You can also use poached, dried fruit this way.

✳ For a more attractive pudding, layer with cream or yoghurt or lightly mix the fruit into the cream to create a marbled effect.

Gooseberry fool

This recipe works equally well with rhubarb.

Serves 2-3

200g (7oz) gooseberries

1 tbsp water

55g (2oz) caster sugar, to taste

100ml (3 1/2 fl oz) ready-made custard

100ml (3 1/2 fl oz) double cream

1 Gently poach the fruit in the water with some of the sugar until soft.

2 Sieve if you want to remove the pips and add extra sugar to taste.

3 Fold the custard into the fruit purée.

4 Cool and then whip the cream and stir into the custard mixture.

Dried fruit fool

If you have dried pears, apples or plums to use up a glut, they make excellent fool ingredients.

Serves 3

285g (10oz) dried fruit, chopped

Orange juice

140ml (5fl oz / 1/4 pint) whipping cream

140ml (5fl oz / 1/4 pint) yoghurt

Optional: Brandy

1 Poach the dried fruit gently in orange juice for about 10 minutes until tender.

2 Purée the fruit, adding extra liquid if required.

3 Whip the cream and then stir in the yoghurt.

4 Stir in the fruit or arrange alternate layers of fruit and cream.

For a more sophisticated dessert, dice a few pieces of whole dried fruit, marinate them in a little brandy and use them to decorate the dish.

Strawberry fool

Serves 2-3

285g (10oz) strawberries

140ml (5fl oz / 1/4 pint) double cream

140ml (5fl oz / 1/4 pint) yoghurt

Optional: Icing sugar

1 Mash the fruit with a fork.

2 Whip the cream.

3 Fold in the yoghurt and crushed fruit.

4 Stir in icing sugar if any extra sweetness is needed.

Strawberry fool is an unusual way to serve strawberries and cream.

VEGETABLE DESSERTS

Some vegetables, such as carrots or squash, are quite sweet and can be used in puddings and cakes as well as in savoury dishes. They are very popular, for example, in Middle Eastern cuisine. The first two recipes, from India and Egypt, produce sweet purées that can be served hot or cold.

Indian carrot pudding

Serves 4

450g (1lb) carrots, grated

850ml (30fl oz / 1¹/₂ pints) milk

200g (7oz) sugar

55g (2oz) butter

30g (1oz) sultanas

1 tsp cardamoms, ground

To garnish:
55g (2oz) chopped nuts, e.g. almonds

1 Warm the milk and sugar and, when dissolved, add the carrots.

2 Bring to the boil and keep at this temperature until the liquid has evaporated – stir regularly as it will take at least 30 minutes and can easily burn.

3 Add the butter and adjust the heat until the mixture begins to fry.

4 Add the sultanas and cook gently for 10-15 minutes before stirring in the cardamom. Cook for a further few minutes, stirring constantly.

5 Garnish with nuts and serve either hot or cold.

Squash and coconut pudding

Serves 4

450g (1lb) squash, peeled, de-seeded, cubed

55g (2oz) sugar

1 tbsp raisins

¹/₄ tbsp desiccated coconut

¹/₄ tbsp blanched almonds, chopped,

¹/₄ tsp cinnamon, ground

¹/₄ tsp allspice

1 Cook the squash in a little water for 10-15 minutes until soft.

2 Drain and then return to the pan and continue heating gently to drive off any remaining water. (If the skin is very tough, bake it in the oven for 30-40 minutes instead and then remove the flesh.)

3 Add the sugar and mash to a purée.

4 Cool and then mix in the rest of the ingredients.

Baked winter squash

Serves 2

1 squash, halved/quartered, de-seeded

3 tbsp butter

85ml (3fl oz) honey

115g (4oz) dried dates/sultanas, chopped

30g (1oz) blanched almonds, chopped

1/2 tsp cinnamon, ground

1/4 tsp nutmeg, ground

1 Cover the squash pieces with foil and bake at 180°C (360°F / Gas Mark 4) for about 30 minutes. Alternativley, to prevent them from drying out, add 1cm (3/8") water to the pan and cook the squash cut-side down.

2 Melt the butter and, off the heat, mix in the rest of the ingredients.

3 Fill the squash cavities with the honey mixture and then bake, uncovered, for another 10-15 minutes until soft.

Winter squash pie

Serves 2

1 butternut/acorn squash, halved, de-seeded

Shortcrust pastry made with 225g (8oz) flour

285ml (10fl oz / 1/2 pint) double cream / evaporated milk

2 eggs, beaten

200g (7oz) light brown sugar

1/2 tsp salt

1 tsp ground cinnamon

1/2 tsp ground ginger

1 Bake the squash at 180°C (360°F / Gas Mark 4) for about 1 hour or until tender.

2 When cool, scrape the flesh off the skin and blend well with the rest of the filling ingredients. You should have about 400g (14oz) squash flesh.

3 Line a deep pie dish with the pastry and bake blind for 10-15 minutes (see page 91).

4 Now add the filling and bake at 200°C (400°F / Gas Mark 6) for 10 minutes.

5 Lower the temperature to 180°C (360°F / Gas Mark 4) and continue cooking for a further 30-40 minutes until the filling is completely set.

ICE CREAMS AND SORBETS

The difference between ice creams and sorbets is the dairy content. Both are delicious on a hot day, but sorbets are particularly refreshing as they contain only ice and sugar and you can even create savoury versions for a sophisticated summer treat.

Ice creams

Ice creams can contain almost anything edible – from broken-up fruit cake or toasted breadcrumbs to tea, coffee, alcohol, nuts, jam and fruit.

There are three basic styles of ice cream you can make:

- Custard-style – which involves first heating egg yolks, sugar and milk. (Replace the yolks with custard powder for anyone who should avoid eating lightly cooked egg.)
- American or simple – which contains no egg and does not require cooking. The main ingredients such as cream, evaporated milk or yoghurt are directly combined with fruit and flavourings and then frozen. Note that, if making your ice cream by hand, this method may not produce such a creamy mix as the custard recipe.
- Water ices – such as sorbets and granitas, which contain no dairy products and are a mixture of sugar syrup and fruit or other flavourings.

Quantities are very flexible and if you want to add extra sweetness just before freezing, use icing or caster sugar as these won't need dissolving first. You can also substitute the listed dairy products in the recipes with others such as Greek or low-fat yoghurt, evaporated or condensed milk or crème fraiche to produce richer or lighter ice creams depending on taste.

Making ice cream

Ice-cream making is much easier with an electric ice-cream maker. With the basic equipment, you first freeze an outer container and then pour your ice cream mixture into an inner bowl that is kept chilled as it is churned. It is perfectly straightforward to make ice cream without using a machine but you will need to take your mixture out of the freezer several times and stir well or blend to break down unwanted ice crystals that will form during the freezing process. However, do not expect the resultant ice cream to be as professionally smooth.

Serving ice cream

We are all familiar with serving scoops of single or mixed flavour ice creams in glass dishes or with your main dessert, but don't forget you can also create parfaits or Knickerbocker Glory – layers of ice cream, fruit, jelly, cream and syrup – or you can make ice-cream cakes. Here ice cream is layered with cake or biscuit crumbs in a tin and frozen until the whole thing has become a single 'cake' that can be turned out and decorated.

* When serving ice cream, always try to let it soften in the fridge for 20-30 minutes before-hand so that it can be easily scooped out and tastes at its best.

Fresh fruit custard-style ice cream

Use about 225-285g (8-10oz) puréed fresh or stewed fruit with the quantities of custard-style ice cream opposite. Try redcurrants, blackcurrants, strawberries, rhubarb, pears, apples, plums or goose-berries mixed with 55-115g (2-4oz) extra sugar if necessary, or combine two or more different fruits such as redcurrant and apple, blackberry and pear, or rhubarb and strawberry.

Note that the flavour lessens after freezing so make your original ice cream mixture quite sweet and strong. Sieve the purée if you don't want any pips or skin.

Basic custard-style ice cream

Serves 4

225ml (8fl oz) milk

225ml (8fl oz) whipping cream / double cream

2 egg yolks, well beaten

140g (5oz) sugar

1-2 tsp vanilla essence

You will also need:
Ice cream maker or freezer-proof container

Blender

....
: ✳ Gelato is slightly
: different from ice cream
: as there is more milk
: than cream and so it
: has a lower fat content.
: If you want to make
: this following the above
: method, use 225ml
: (8fl oz) milk and 115ml
: (4fl oz) cream plus 2 egg
: yolks and 55g (2oz)
: sugar, and make sure
: you sieve the mixture
: before adding the fruit.
....

1   Place a pan of milk inside a saucepan half-filled with water (or use a double boiler) and heat the milk gently.

2   Whisk the sugar and egg yolks together in a bowl and stir in the warm milk.

3   Return the mixture to the heat and stir gently until it thickens – it should coat the back of a spoon. Do *not* allow it to boil or it will curdle.

4   Remove from the heat and stir in the vanilla.

5   Strain and then allow to cool.

6   Stir in the cream together with your chosen fruit purée (see the 'Fresh fruit custard-style ice cream' recipe opposite for details) and any other ingredients.

7   Use an ice-cream maker according to the instructions.

Or:

Pour the mixture into a freezer-proof container.

Stir well and then freeze for about 40 minutes. Take the mixture out of the freezer and mix in the frozen sections that will have started to freeze around the edges. You can use a fork or blender. Now freeze again for an hour. Repeat this process 2 or 3 times before leaving the ice cream to set firm.

Carrot ice cream

Just as carrots make good cakes, so their sweetness makes them an unusual ice cream ingredient. Some recipes use carrot juice, but you can also liquidise and sieve cooked carrots and add these to a basic custard. You could also try mixing them with cream or mascarpone cheese instead. In Italy, a popular ice cream called Ace is made from carrots, oranges and lemons.

If you don't have any carrots, you could try substituting butternut squash.

Serves 4

225g (8oz) carrots, chopped

4-6 tbsp orange juice (or mix orange and lemon)

140ml (5fl oz / 1/4 pint) milk / single cream

140ml (5fl oz / 1/4 pint) double cream

1-2 drops vanilla essence

1/2 tsp ground cinnamon

2 egg yolks

50g (1.75oz) sugar

You will also need:
Ice-cream maker or freezer-proof container

Blender

1   Gently cook the carrots in a little water, liquidise and then leave to cool.

2   Whisk the egg yolks and sugar together in a bowl.

3   Very gently warm the rest of the ingredients except the fruit juice in a saucepan over hot water and then remove from the heat.

4   Pour half the warmed cream mixture on to the eggs. Whisk and then return to the pan with the rest of the warmed cream.

5   Gently stir the mixture over hot water until it starts to thicken. Remove immediately from the heat.

6   Stir the carrot purée into the ice-cream mixture together with the fruit juice and extra sugar to taste.

7   Strain the mixture and then use an ice-cream maker or follow the manual freezing method on page 155.

For a carrot glut, why not try ice cream for a change?

Easy fruit ice cream

Serves 4

450g (1lb) soft fruit such as strawberries, raspberries, blackcurrants
or stewed plums

340ml (12fl oz) whipping cream /
double cream

225g (8oz) caster sugar, or to taste

Optional:
1 tbsp lemon juice

You will also need:
Ice-cream maker or
freezer-proof container

Blender

1 Liquidise or mash the fruit and mix with the
   sugar. Add more if the mixture is not sweet
   enough.

2 Lightly whip the cream.

3 Add the fruit and beat until well blended.
   Add lemon juice if you prefer your ice cream
   a little tart.

4 Use an ice-cream maker according to the
   instructions, or pour the mixture into a
   freezer-proof container and follow the
   manual freezing method described on
   page 155.

Frozen fruit yoghurt

Serves 4

285g (10oz) soft fruit

115g (4oz) icing or caster sugar

285ml (10fl oz / 1/2 pint) plain
yoghurt

Other flavourings, e.g. lemon or
orange juice

You will also need:
Ice-cream maker or
freezer-proof container

Blender

1 Purée the fruit together with the sugar in a
   blender.

2 Add any extra flavourings to taste.

3 Add the yoghurt and blend until smooth.

4 Use an ice-cream maker according to
   instructions, or follow the manual freezing
   method described on page 155.

Sweet sorbets

Any fruit can be turned into a sorbet, but the most common versions use citrus fruits either entirely or added to orchard fruit or berries for a more zingy flavour.

Fruit water ice (sorbet)

Serves 4

510g (1lb 2oz) fruit e.g. straw-berries or blackcurrants

115g (4oz) sugar

115ml (4fl oz) water

Optional:
1 egg white

2 tbsp concentrated orange juice

You will also need:
Ice cream maker or freezer-proof container

Blender

1   Dissolve the sugar in boiling water and simmer to make a syrup.

2   Cool and then add the fruit. (For fruit such as rhubarb or gooseberries, simmer with the sugar or use previously stewed fruit.)

3   Liquidise and, if preferred, sieve to remove any pips.

4   Add the orange juice for a different flavour and add extra sugar if necessary.

5   Follow the manual freezing method on page 155 or use an ice-cream maker according to instructions.

6   For a creamier, less grainy texture, remove the semi-frozen sorbet mixture from the freezer and fold in the whisked egg white before returning to the freezer.

7   For a granita, leave the mixture to freeze without extra mixing to allow ice crystals to form. Just before serving, break up the ice with a fork.

Plum and orange sorbet

Serves 4

155g (5 1/2 oz) plums, pitted

3 tbsp sugar

255ml (9fl oz) orange juice

Optional: Orange zest

You will also need: Blender

1   Blend all the ingredients until smooth. The plum skins will give the sorbet a spotty appearance so you may prefer to skin the fruit first.

2   Follow the manual freezing method on page 155 or use an ice-cream maker to create the sorbet.

3   Leave out to soften and blend again just before serving.

Savoury sorbets

You can make savoury sorbets such as tomato, cucumber or Gazpacho-style (cucumber, tomato and peppers), which can be served as a summer starter or a palate-clearing course at a dinner party.

Gazpacho sorbet

Serves 4

2 large tomatoes, peeled, coarsely chopped

2 red peppers, peeled, de-seeded, chopped

1/2 cucumber, peeled, de-seeded, chopped

1/4 red onion, peeled, chopped

1 garlic clove, peeled, chopped

4 tsp red wine vinegar

1/2 tsp hot sauce, e.g. Tabasco

Salt to taste

30g (1oz) sugar

To serve: Cucumber slices; Basil leaves; Olive oil

You will also need: Blender; Ice-cream maker or freezer-proof container

1 Combine the vegetables with the rest of the ingredients and, ideally, leave for a few hours to allow the flavours to develop.

2 Blend the mixture until smooth and then strain through a sieve.

3 Follow the manual freezing method on page 155 or use an ice-cream maker to create the sorbet.

4 To serve, place scoops of sorbet on a bed of thinly sliced cucumber drizzled with olive oil and garnished with torn basil leaves.

Tomato sorbet

Serves 4-6

115g (4oz) sugar

115ml (4fl oz) water

6-8 ripe tomatoes

Lemon juice

170ml (6fl oz) tomato juice

Dash of Tabasco or Worcester sauce

Herbs, e.g. basil or chives, chopped

Salt and pepper

You will also need: Blender; Ice-cream maker or freezer-proof container

1 Dissolve the sugar in the water.

2 Cool and then add all the other ingredients.

3 Liquidise and season to taste.

4 Follow the manual freezing method or use an ice-cream maker.

Chapter 7
Bread and cakes

CAKES

Upside-down cakes

Vegetable cakes

BREADS AND TEA BREADS

Breads

Tea breads

CAKES

You can add fresh fruit to any cake mix, although you have to be careful that it doesn't produce so much water that it stops the cake mixture cooking properly. British 'fruit' cakes are normally made with bought dried fruit such as raisins, sultanas and peel. Once you have tried fruit drying (see Chapter 10) you can add your own dried pears, apples and plums chopped into small pieces to make a very rich and flavoursome cake.

Old-fashioned fruit cake

225g (8oz) mixed dried fruit

225g (8oz) self-raising flour

2 eggs, beaten

115g (4oz) butter

115g (4oz) sugar

Grated zest of 1 orange

Grated zest of 1 lemon

1/4 tsp salt

1/2 tsp mixed spice

2 tbsp milk

1. Cream the fat and sugar together.
2. Stir in the eggs.
3. Fold in the fruit, zest, salt, spices and flour.
4. Add the milk and mix well.
5. Turn into a greased baking tin and bake at 180°C (360°F / Gas Mark 4) for about 1-1 1/2 hours.
6. Test that it is done by making sure a knife or skewer comes out cleanly. Leave in the tin for about 10 minutes and then turn out to cool.

Dorset apple cake

This cake is commonly served warm with double or clotted cream as a dessert, but it is also excellent as a conventional cake.

225g (8oz) cooking apples, peeled, cored and chopped (plus extra slices for a topping)

225g (8oz) plain flour

1¹/₂ tsp baking powder

115g (4oz) butter

155g (5 ¹/₂ oz) soft light brown sugar

1 egg, beaten

1 tbsp lemon juice

¹/₂ tsp cinnamon, ground / mixed spice

2-3 tbsp milk

1   Sift the flour and baking powder together.

2   Rub in the butter so that the mixture resembles breadcrumbs.

3   Stir in the egg, lemon juice, 115g (4oz) sugar and apple pieces.

4   Add a little milk and mix to a soft, dropping consistency.

5   Turn into a greased tin.

6   If you want to, arrange sliced apple pieces over the cake mixture.

7   Mix together the rest of the sugar with the cinnamon or mixed spice and sprinkle over the top of the cake.

8   Bake at 180°C (360°F / Gas Mark 4) for about 40 minutes until a knife test shows that it is done.

9   Leave to cool in the tin for 5-10 minutes and then turn out on to a wire rack.

Dorset apple cake – full of moist fruit pieces.

Blackberry cakes

Makes 10-12 individual cakes

30g (1oz) plain flour

130g (4 1/2 oz) icing sugar

85g (3oz) ground almonds

85g (3oz) butter

3 egg whites, whisked to soft peaks

Grated lemon zest

85g (3oz) blackberries

To serve: Icing sugar

You will also need:
Individual paper cake cases / muffin tins

1   Melt the butter and then leave to cool.

2   Mix the flour and icing sugar together with the almonds.

3   Make a well in the centre and stir in the egg whites, lemon zest and melted butter.

4   Spoon the mixture into individual paper cake cases or greased muffin tins and sprinkle a few blackberries into each one.

5   Bake at 190°C (380°F / Gas Mark 5) for about 20 minutes until puffed up and golden brown.

6   To serve, turn out and dust lightly with icing sugar.

Plum cake

225g (8oz) plums, stoned and chopped

225g (8oz) self-raising flour

100g (3 1/2 oz) butter

55g (2oz) sultanas/raisins

85g (3oz) soft brown sugar

2 large eggs, beaten

4 tbsp golden syrup

1-2 tbsp extra brown sugar

1 tsp ground cinnamon

1   Rub the butter into the flour.

2   Stir in the dried fruit and sugar.

3   Mix the eggs and syrup together and add to the cake mix together with the plums.

4   Transfer to a greased baking tin and top with a good sprinkle of sugar mixed with the cinnamon.

5   Bake at 180°C (360°F / Gas Mark 4) for 40-50 minutes and then leave to cool completely before turning out on to a wire rack.

✽ If you ever find it hard to turn out a cake cleanly when it contains soft fruit such as plums, serve it as a pudding straight from the baking tin.

Gooseberry cake

285g (10oz) gooseberries, topped and tailed

100g (3 1/2 oz) butter

140g (5oz) sugar

85ml (3fl oz) yoghurt

2 eggs

155g (5 1/2 oz) plain flour

1 tsp baking powder

4 tbsp golden syrup

1   Cream the sugar with 85g (3oz) of the butter.

2   Beat in the yoghurt and eggs and then fold in the flour and baking powder.

3   Place the mix in a greased cake tin and bake at 180°C (360°F / Gas Mark 4) for 20 minutes.

4   Meanwhile, melt the remaining butter with the golden syrup.

5   Add the gooseberries to the pan and mix well, allowing the gooseberries to soften slightly.

6   Remove the cake from the oven, pour over the gooseberry mix and then continue baking for a further 30 minutes, or until risen and golden.

Raspberry and nut tray bake

225 (8oz) raspberries

225g (8oz) plain flour

225g (8oz) porridge oats

225g (8oz) butter

170g (6oz) light brown sugar

100g (3 1/2 oz) pine nuts / blanched almonds

1   Mix the flour, oats and butter together with your fingers to make crumbs.

2   Mix in three-quarters of the nuts and all the sugar.

3   Spread two-thirds of the mixture in a greased baking tin.

4   Scatter over the raspberries and then spoon the rest of the mixture over the top of the fruit.

5   Finish off by sprinkling over the rest of the nuts.

6   Press down very lightly and bake at 190°C (380°F / Gas Mark 5) for 35-40 minutes until golden on top.

7   Cut into bars whilst still hot but leave to cool before removing from the tin.

Mixed fruit muffins

This is an excellent way to use up fruit pulp left over from making jellies or cordials, but you can also use fresh fruit such as blackcurrants, blackberries, finely diced plums or raspberries in the normal way.

Makes 12 muffins

100g (3 1/2 oz) sugar

185g (6 1/2 oz) plain flour

2 tsp baking powder

1/4 tsp salt

100ml (3 1/2 fl oz) milk

55ml (2fl oz) vegetable oil

1 egg

85-115g (3-4oz) fruit pulp / mixed fruit

Optional:
1/2 tsp flavouring, e.g. vanilla/ cinnamon

You will also need:
12 paper cases / individual muffin tins

1 Prepare 12 muffin tins and pre-heat the oven to 200°C (400°F / Gas Mark 6).

2 Sift together the flour, salt and baking powder.

3 Make a well in the centre of the bowl.

4 Beat together the egg, sugar, milk and oil and then pour into the dry ingredients in the bowl. Mix just enough to combine all the ingredients and make sure there is no flour left unmixed at the bottom of the bowl.

5 Fold in the fruit and immediately spoon the mixture into paper cases or individual muffin tins.

6 Bake for 20-25 minutes.

✱ The most important thing to remember when making muffins is that after combining the wet and dry ingredients they should be mixed as little as possible. If the ingredients are beaten or over-stirred, the muffins will become tough and heavy.

Upside-down cakes

If you arrange a layer of fruit slices such as apples, plums or pears over the base of a cake tin and then spoon over any suitable cake mix, you will have an attractive topping already in place when you turn out the cake.

Toffee apple upside-down cake

140g (5oz) butter

140g (5oz) dark brown sugar

2 eating apples, peeled, sliced thinly

2 eggs

1/2 tsp vanilla essence

1 tsp cinnamon or nutmeg

140g (5oz) self-raising flour

1-2 tbsp milk

To serve:
Custard/cream

1   Grease and line a baking tin, preferably one with a loose base.

2   Melt 30g (1oz) butter and 30g (1oz) sugar together and pour into the tin.

3   Arrange the apple in a neat layer over the sugar mixture.

4   Cream together the rest of the sugar and butter and then beat in the eggs and vanilla essence.

5   Fold in the flour and spices, adding milk if necessary for a dropping consistency.

6   Spoon this mixture over the apple slices and bake at 180°C (360°F / Gas Mark 4) for 40 minutes or until cooked when tested with a skewer or knife.

7   When cool, turn out on to a plate so the apple slices are at the top and either slice or serve warm with custard or cream.

Pear upside-down cake

2-3 pears, peeled, cored, halved/sliced

40g (1 1/2 oz) melted butter

1 tsp cinnamon

100g (3 1/2 oz) brown sugar

Cake mix:
170g (6oz) butter

3 eggs

170g (6oz) self-raising flour

170g (6oz) sugar

5-6 tbsp milk

Optional:
1-2 drops vanilla essence / 1/4 tsp ginger, ground

1　Grease a baking tin that is lined with baking parchment.

2　Mix the melted butter and brown sugar together, stir in the cinnamon and then pour this mixture into the tin. Arrange the pear slices on top in a star shape, cut-sides down.

3　Cream the butter and sugar and then beat in the eggs. Add vanilla essence at this stage, if using.

4　Fold in the flour and any ground spices and add milk for a smooth batter.

5　Spoon over the pears and level the top.

6　Bake at 180°C (360°F / Gas Mark 4) for about 40 minutes until completely cooked.

7　Leave to cool fully before turning out and gently peeling away the baking paper.

Vegetable cakes

Strangely enough, vegetables such as carrots, winter squash, courgettes and beetroot also make good cake ingredients. You won't recognise the taste of the vegetables but the cakes will be moist and fruity and keep very well. Carrots probably make the best cakes as both squash and courgettes have a rather milder flavour. Beetroot is delicious with chocolate but if you want to experiment with other cake recipes, take care with the amount of beetroot as too much may make your cakes taste earthy.

＊ Before adding grated vegetables to cake mix, gently squeeze out the mixture and pat dry so that you remove excess moisture.

Beetroot and chocolate cake

200g (7oz) plain chocolate, broken up

2 large eggs

170g (6oz) light brown sugar

85ml (3fl oz) sunflower oil

1 tsp vanilla extract

85g (3oz) self-raising flour

1/2 tsp baking powder

1/2 tsp bicarbonate of soda

40g (1 1/2 oz) ground almonds

200g (7oz) raw beetroot, peeled and grated

Icing:

155g (5 1/2 oz) plain chocolate

100g (3 1/2 oz) icing sugar

100ml (3 1/2 fl oz) soured cream

1 Melt the chocolate in a microwave or over a pan of hot water and leave to cool.

2 Whisk the eggs, sugar and oil until smooth and creamy. Stir in the vanilla extract and then fold in the flour, baking powder, bicarbonate of soda and almonds.

3 Add the beetroot and melted chocolate and mix well.

4 Pour the mixture into a well-oiled tin and bake at 180°C (360°F / Gas Mark 4) for about 1 hour.

5 Test that it is cooked and then leave to cool in the tin for 10 minutes before turning out.

6 Make the icing by melting the chocolate and leaving it to cool. Then beat in the sugar and cream and ice the cake when it is cold.

Courgette and chocolate cake

3 eggs

55ml (2fl oz) vegetable oil

100ml (3 1/2 fl oz) milk

255g (9oz) soft brown sugar

255g (9oz) plain flour

55g (2oz) cocoa

1 tsp baking powder

1 tsp bicarbonate of soda

225g (8oz) courgettes, grated

1 Mix the eggs and sugar in a bowl and beat until they are pale and fluffy.

2 Add the oil and milk and mix well.

3 Stir in the grated courgettes.

4 In a separate bowl, mix the flour, cocoa, baking powder and bicarbonate of soda and stir until blended well together.

5 Fold the dry ingredients into the egg mixture.

6 Bake at 180°C (360°F / Gas Mark 4) for 40-45 minutes.

7 Leave to cool in the tin and then turn on to a wire rack.

Carrot cake

This cake makes an excellent hot pudding served with cream or custard, but it is usually served with a cream cheese icing. To stop the topping going runny, keep it in the fridge until the cake is ready to serve. Or you could top it with normal butter cream or glacé icing, flavoured with vanilla, orange or lemon.

Cake mix:
115g (4oz) butter
115g (4oz) brown sugar
2 eggs, beaten
225g (8oz) carrots, grated
285g (10oz) dried fruit
170g (6oz) plain flour
Pinch of salt
1 tsp baking powder
1 tsp nutmeg, ground
1 tsp cinnamon, ground
Optional:
30-55g (1-2oz) chopped walnuts
Icing:
155g (5 1/2 oz) butter
400g (14oz) cream cheese
200g (7oz) icing sugar, sifted
Flavouring, e.g. vanilla essence

1 To make the cake, cream the butter and sugar and beat in the eggs.
2 Mix in the carrots, nuts (if using) and fruit.
3 Fold in the dry ingredients.
4 Bake in a well greased loaf tin at 180°C (360°F / Gas Mark 4) for about 45 minutes, or until a knife comes out cleanly.
5 For the topping, cream together the butter and cream cheese and then beat in the sugar gradually. Add the flavouring and beat until thick and fluffy.
6 Spread the icing over the top and sides of the cake and decorate with extra walnuts.

✽ When using a soft icing like cream cheese, keep both the cake and icing cold and the cake will be easier to ice.

Courgette cake

225g (8oz) courgettes, grated

100g (3 1/2 oz) sultanas

4 tbsp orange juice

3 eggs

170ml (6fl oz) vegetable oil

200g (7oz) light brown sugar

225g (8oz) self-raising flour

1/2 tsp baking powder

1/2 tsp bicarbonate of soda

55g (2oz) almonds, toasted and chopped

1 Put the sultanas in a saucepan with the orange juice. Bring to the boil and simmer for 5 minutes until the raisins have absorbed all the liquid, taking care they don't burn. (Alternatively, soak the sultanas in orange juice for an hour or so before baking.)

2 Combine the eggs, oil and sugar in a large bowl and mix well.

3 Fold in the flour, baking powder, bicarbonate of soda, almonds, courgettes and sultanas.

4 Spoon into a greased cake tin and bake at 180°C (360°F / Gas Mark 4) for 45-50 minutes.

* You could also use this mixture to make muffins. Spoon into greased muffin cases and bake for 25-30 minutes.

Butternut squash cup cakes

1/2 butternut squash (roughly 255g [9oz]), peeled, de-seeded

155g (5 1/2 oz) self-raising flour

155g (5 1/2 oz) light brown sugar

100g (3 1/2 oz) butter, melted

2 eggs

85g (3oz) sultanas

1 tsp bicarbonate of soda

1 tbsp orange juice

1-2 tsp spice, e.g. ginger, mixed spice or cinnamon

Topping:
30g (1oz) sugar

1-2 tbsp orange juice

You will also need:
Individual paper cake cases / muffin tins

1 Grate the squash or use a food processor to grind up fairly finely.

2 In a bowl, combine the flour, sugar, bicarbonate, spices and sultanas.

3 Beat the eggs and stir in with the melted butter.

4 Add the squash and orange juice and mix well.

5 Spoon into prepared muffin tins or paper cases and bake at 180°C (360°F / Gas Mark 4) for about 20 minutes.

6 For the topping, dissolve the sugar in hot orange juice to make a syrup. Pierce holes in the cakes and, whilst still hot, spoon over the syrup. When cool, the cakes will have a crunchy sugary topping.

BREADS AND TEA BREADS

The difference between bread and tea bread is that bread is normally made with strong bread flour and yeast to ensure that the dough rises. The pizza dough on page 115 makes a wonderful loaf of white bread, and you can add a wide range of different ingredients, such as nuts, olives, herbs, dried fruit or grated or chopped vegetables, or even replace some of the flour with  grated vegetables. However, any strongly flavoured additions will limit what you can eat with your bread. For example, tomato flatbread is delicious with cheese, salad and eggs but not very nice with jam!

Breads

For a delicious nutty, wholemeal loaf, just substitute 225g (8oz) white flour in the pizza dough recipe (page 115) for strong wholemeal or speciality bread flour such as granary. Otherwise, try one of the following recipes as a way to use up a glut of fruit or vegetables.

Courgette bread

450g (1lb) courgettes, grated

540g (1lb 3oz) strong white bread flour (or 3/4 white, 1/4 wholemeal)

1 sachet (7g / 1/4 oz) instant dried yeast

4 tbsp cheese, e.g. Cheddar or Parmesan, grated

2 tbs vegetable oil

1 tsp salt

200ml (7fl oz) hand-hot water

Sunflower seeds

You will also need: 1lb loaf tin

1 Dry the courgettes very well.

2 Combine all the ingredients except the seeds in a bowl and mix into a soft dough. Add a little more water if necessary.

3 Knead for several minutes and then cover and leave for about an hour to double in size.

4 Knead again and place in a 1lb (450g) greased loaf tin.

5 Scatter sunflower seeds over the top.

6 Cover and leave for another hour and then bake at 200°C (400°F / Gas Mark 6) for about 35 minutes until the bottom sounds hollow when tapped. Cool on a wire rack.

Carrot and raisin loaf

This is one of the few types of bread that is made without yeast, so is very quick and easy. You may find it quite heavy, but the crust is delicious and it makes excellent toast. It also goes well with cheese, salad or cold meat.

140g (5oz) carrots, grated

55g (2oz) raisins/sultanas

510g (1lb 2oz) plain flour

2 tsp bicarbonate of soda

1 tsp salt

30g (1oz) walnuts, chopped

285ml (10fl oz / 1/2 pint) plain yoghurt

100ml (3 1/2 fl oz) milk

Optional:
Substitute 140g (5oz) plain flour with wholemeal flour

You will also need: 1lb loaf tin

1   Mix the flour, soda and salt in a bowl and fold in the carrots, fruit, carrots, nuts and yoghurt.

2   Add enough milk to make a soft, slightly sticky dough.

3   Turn into a 1lb (450g) greased loaf tin and bake at 220°C (430°F / Gas Mark 7) for about 45 minutes. Tap the base to check it sounds hollow.

Apple bread

Make this dough quite wet (it will be impossible to knead) for bread with a lovely light, spongy texture with just a hint of apple. Serve it with cheese or pork slices for a perfect lunch.

225g (8oz) apple purée (requires 1-2 cooking apples)

1 sachet (7g / 1/4 oz) instant dried yeast

450g (1lb) strong white flour or 3/4 white, 1/4 wholemeal

1/2 tsp salt

200-285ml (7-10fl oz / 1/3- 1/2 pint) warm water

To glaze: Milk/flour

You will also need: baking sheet / 1lb loaf tin

1   Make a thick, dry, unsweetened apple purée with cooking apples and leave to cool. (Ideally use a microwave so there is no danger of the purée drying out.)

2   Mix all the ingredients together, including the apple purée, and combine with enough water to make a soft dough.

3   Knead for several minutes and then cover and leave for 1 hour to double in size.

4   Knock back and knead again. Shape into a round loaf and place on a greased baking sheet (or use a 1lb [450g] greased loaf tin).

5   Cover and leave for another hour.

6   Glaze with milk or shake on some flour.

7   Bake in a hot oven at 200°C (400°F / Gas Mark 6) for about 40 minutes.

8   When the base sounds hollow when tapped, leave to cool on a wire rack.

Tomato flatbread

This recipe uses tomatoes that have been dried and stored in oil
(see page 221), as fresh tomatoes would be far too wet.

510g (1lb 2oz) strong white
bread flour

1 tsp salt

2 tbsp olive oil

50g (1.75oz) Parmesan cheese,
grated

50g (1.75oz) dried tomatoes in oil,
chopped and drained

3 tbsp tomato paste

2 tbsp herbs, e.g. rosemary

1 sachet (7g / 1/4 oz) instant
dried yeast

340ml (12fl oz) hand-hot water

Extra salt and pepper

You will also need:
9" round tin

1. Place all the ingredients except the water in a bowl.

2. Pour in the water, mix together, and then knead to a soft dough. Don't use quite all the water at first, but add until the mixture is the right consistency. As you will be transferring it straight to a tin, you can afford to have a wetter mixture than for normal bread.

3. Press into a greased 9" (23cm) round tin and flatten with your hands.

4. Use your thumb to press indentations into the surface.

5. Sprinkle with a little oil from the tomatoes, salt, black pepper and extra herbs.

6. Cover with a plastic bag and leave to prove for about 1 hour.

7. Bake at 200°C (400°F / Gas Mark 6) for about 40 minutes.

This bread works
especially well in
tomato bruschetta
(see page 48).

Tea breads

These are more like cakes than bread, although they usually contain less egg and sugar. They use baking powder or bicarbonate of soda as the rising agent and keep well. They are often served in buttered slices as they are not normally iced.

Courgette tea bread

170g (6oz) courgettes, grated
1 large egg
85ml (3fl oz) vegetable oil
155g (5 1/2 oz) plain flour
1/2 tsp baking powder
1 tsp bicarbonate of soda
170g (6oz) dark brown sugar
1 tsp cinnamon
80g (2.75oz) sultanas/raisins
30g (1oz) walnuts, chopped
You will also need: 1lb loaf tin

1 Gently squeeze out any moisture from the courgettes and then combine them with the dry ingredients in a bowl.

2 Beat the egg with the oil, add to the bowl and mix into a soft batter.

3 Pour into a 1lb (450g) greased and lined loaf tin and bake at 180°C (360°F / Gas Mark 4) for about 1 hour until cooked through when tested with a knife or skewer.

4 Leave to cool in the tin before turning out.

Pear tea bread

2 pears, peeled and grated
1 pear, peeled and mashed
1 egg
2 tbsp water
1/2 tsp vanilla essence
200g (7oz) plain flour
200g (7oz) sugar
1 tsp cinnamon
1/2 tsp bicarbonate of soda
1/4 tsp baking powder
1/4 tsp salt
You will also need: 1lb loaf tin

1 Mix the pears, water, egg and vanilla in a bowl.

2 In a separate bowl, combine the dry ingredients and then stir the wet into the dry mixture fairly rapidly.

3 Transfer to a greased 1lb (450g) loaf tin and bake at 180°C (360°F / Gas Mark 4) for an hour.

4 Test that the tea bread is completely cooked and then cool on a rack.

Winter squash tea bread

255g (9oz) squash flesh, cooked

40g (1 1/2 oz) walnuts, chopped (can be toasted first)

450g (1lb) strong plain bread flour

300g (10 1/2 oz) brown sugar

1 tsp bicarbonate of soda

1/2 tsp salt

1 tsp nutmeg

1 tsp cinnamon

100g (3 1/2 oz) butter, melted

approx. 55ml (2fl oz) milk

Optional:
55g (2oz) raisins

You will also need: 1lb loaf tin

1   Mix the sugar, flour, soda, salt and spices together in a bowl.

2   Stir in the squash, nuts and butter and add enough milk to make a soft mixture.

3   If you like dried fruit in your tea bread, add the raisins.

4   Turn into a 1lb (450g) greased loaf tin and bake at 170°C (340°F / Gas Mark 3) for about 1 hour until a knife comes out cleanly.

5   Leave to cool on a wire rack.

Apple and raisin tea bread

225g (8oz) plain flour

225g (8oz) sugar

1 tsp baking powder

1 tsp bicarbonate of soda

Pinch of salt

1 tsp cinnamon, ground

1/2 tsp nutmeg, grated

115ml (4fl oz) milk

30g (1oz) butter, melted

1 egg, beaten

115g (4oz) grated apple

55g (2oz) raisins

55g (2oz) walnuts, chopped

You will also need: 1lb loaf tin

1   Mix the dry ingredients in a bowl.

2   Make a well in the centre and pour in the milk, melted butter and egg. Combine these together well.

3   Stir in the fruit and nuts.

4   Turn into a 1lb (450g) greased loaf tin and bake at 180°C (360°F / Gas Mark 4) for about 1 hour until a knife comes out clean.

5   Cool on a wire rack.

Chapter 8
Preserves

CHUTNEYS

RELISHES

SALSAS

PICKLES

Picked vegetables

Pickled fruit

JAMS

JELLIES

FRUIT CHEESES AND BUTTERS

MINCEMEAT 204

VEGETABLE PRESERVES

CANDIED FRUIT 207

CHUTNEYS

Chutneys, which come originally from India, tend to be fruit-based or use fruit and vegetable combinations and they range from the mild to the very hot. They are usually quite thick and are the perfect accompaniment to hot dishes, such as curry or chilli con carne, as well as making an excellent addition to cheese or ham sandwiches.

Chutneys are a particularly good way to preserve any under-ripe fruit, such as tomatoes or pears, that you may need to pick early to avoid frost damage. Here they are usually combined with apples and cooked with brown rather than white sugar.

There are no set rules as to how to spice up your chutneys, so you can add a wide range of flavourings to a basic fruit or vegetable mix – including whole curry spices, dried herbs, onion or mustard seeds, ginger, dried fruit, chillies or garlic. Another way to vary the flavour is to use different vinegar.

When making anything like chutneys (or relishes) that include vinegar, it is important not to use a copper pan as the vinegar will react with the metal. You should also make sure that the lids of your jars are glass or plastic-coated.

Most of the recipes in this section will make about 4-6 jars of chutney.

Sterilising jars for chutney

You must always use sterilised jars when preserving food products. For chutney, relishes or pickles, use containers with rubber seals and metal clips such as Kilner jars if you have them, or old jam jars.

- Wash the jars thoroughly in hot water.
- Heat them in the oven at 150°C (300°F / Gas Mark 2) for 15 minutes.
- Keep them hot if pouring in hot liquids, to prevent the glass cracking.
- Leave a small space at the top when pouring in the chutney or pickling vinegar, so the contents do not touch the lid.

You can also store chutney (but only chutney) in plastic containers in the freezer.

Cooking apple chutney

1kg (2lb 3oz) cooking apples, cored, peeled and chopped

285ml (10fl oz / 1/2 pint) distilled vinegar

2 cloves garlic, crushed

340g (12oz) brown sugar

1 level tsp ginger, ground

1/2 level tsp mixed spice

Pinch of cayenne pepper

1/4 level tsp salt

1 Cook the apples with the garlic and half the vinegar for 15-20 minutes.

2 Add the other ingredients and cook until thick and rich-looking.

3 Put into hot, clean, sterilised jars. Seal and label.

* Ideally, leave chutneys to mature for several months before using them, as this gives the flavours time to develop.

Beetroot and apple chutney

Many people replace the lemon with orange juice to make beetroot and orange chutney.

900g (2lb) beetroot, grated

450g (1lb) onions, chopped

450g (1lb) cooking apples, peeled and chopped

225g (8oz) raisins

450g (1lb) sugar

570ml (20fl oz / 1 pint) distilled vinegar

2 tbs ground ginger

40g (1.5oz) salt

3-4 tbsp lemon juice

1 Warm the sugar in the vinegar until it dissolves.

2 Add the rest of the ingredients, bring to the boil and then simmer for 1 hour or until thick.

3 Bottle in hot, sterilised jars. Seal and label.

Courgette chutney

900g (2lb) courgettes, chopped

1 large onion, chopped

1 large cooking apple, chopped

1 garlic clove, crushed

255g (9oz) dark brown sugar

285ml (10fl oz / 1/2 pint) white wine vinegar

1/2 tsp salt

Optional:
Ginger root, chopped

Chillies

Mustard seeds

1. Place all the ingredients in a large pan.
2. Bring to the boil and then simmer for about 1 hour or until thick.
3. Add to clean, hot, sterilised jars. Seal and label.

> ✱ For a colourful summer chutney, replace 115g (4oz) courgettes with chopped tomatoes.

Runner bean chutney

900g (2lb) runner beans, sliced

4-5 onions, chopped

680g (1lb 8oz) demerara sugar

850ml (30fl oz / 11/2 pints) distilled vinegar

11/2 tbsp turmeric

11/2 tbsp dry mustard powder

11/2 tbsp cornflour, mixed with a little vinegar

1. Cook the beans and onions in salted water until just tender but still crunchy.
2. Drain well.
3. Bring the vinegar and sugar to the boil and then simmer to dissolve the sugar.
4. Add the vegetables and spices and cook for 20 minutes.
5. Stir in the flour mixture and cook for a further 10 minutes or so until the chutney has thickened.
6. Cool and then add to clean, hot, sterilised jars. Seal and label.

Spiced pear chutney

1.1-1.3kg (2lb 8oz-3lb) pears, peeled, cored and chopped

2 cooking apples, peeled, cored and chopped

450g (1lb) onions, chopped

450g (1lb) seedless raisins

1 tsp hot chilli powder

1 tsp ginger, ground

1 garlic clove, crushed

1 tsp salt

1/2 tsp nutmeg

450g (1lb) soft brown sugar

570ml (20fl oz / 1 pint) white distilled vinegar

1. Place all the ingredients in a pan, stir and bring to the boil

2. Simmer, stirring regularly, for 1 hour or until thick and syrupy.

3. Ladle into hot, clean, sterilised jars. Seal and label.

Plum and apple chutney

900g-1.3kg (2lb -3lb) plums, stoned and chopped

450g (1lb) apples, cored and chopped

2 onions, chopped

3 garlic cloves, crushed

2 heaped tsp ginger

450g (1lb) raisins

225g (8oz) soft dark sugar

225g (8oz) demerara sugar

570ml (20fl oz / 1 pint) malt vinegar / cider vinegar

2 tsp salt

2 cinnamon sticks

30g (1oz) allspice berries

3-4 whole cloves

1. Tie the whole spices in muslin and suspend the bag tied to the handle inside the pan.

2. Add all the ingredients and stir well.

3. Bring to the boil and then simmer for 1-2 hours, stirring regularly to avoid burning, until the chutney is thick and pulpy.

4. Remove the bag of spices.

5. Fill sterilised jars with the chutney. Seal and label.

Tomato and sultana chutney

140ml (5fl oz / 1/4 pint) white wine vinegar

155g (5 1/2 oz) sugar

55g (2oz) sultanas

510g (1lb 2oz) ripe tomatoes, washed, roughly chopped

1 large onion, diced

1 garlic clove, crushed

Spices, e.g. cardamom pods and coriander seeds

2-3 bay leaves

1 tsp thyme, chopped

To season:
Salt and pepper

Optional:
2 tbsp tomato purée for extra colour and strength

Red chilli / ginger, finely chopped

Substitute sugar with brown sugar for a darker colour

1 Warm the vinegar, sugar and spices over a low heat first to dissolve the sugar.

2 Bring to the boil and boil for about 5 minutes so that it becomes more syrupy.

3 Add the chopped tomatoes, bay, sultanas, onion, garlic and, if using, the tomato purée, chilli and ginger.

4 Bring back to the boil and then reduce the heat to a gentle simmer.

5 Cook for about 30-40 minutes, stirring regularly, until the chutney has thickened.

6 Add the chopped thyme, season and pot in sterilised containers. Seal and label.

Both ripe and green tomatoes make excellent chutneys.

Green tomato chutney

1.5kg (3lb 5oz) green tomatoes, chopped

450g (1lb) cooking apples, peeled, cored and chopped

450g (1lb) onions, chopped

225g (8oz) sultanas/raisins, chopped

1 tbsp salt

450g (1lb) light brown sugar

Spices, e.g. ground ginger, mustard, curry powder

570ml (20fl oz / 1 pint) malt vinegar / cider vinegar

Optional:
115g (4oz) chillies, chopped

1 Place the onions and tomatoes in a bowl and stir in the salt. Cover and leave overnight to draw out the water and enhance the flavours.

2 Place the vinegar and sugar in a pan, bring to the boil, and then simmer until the sugar has dissolved.

3 Strain but don't rinse the tomatoes and onions, and add to the pan with the other ingredients.

4 Simmer for about 1 hour, stirring occasionally, until a thick consistency has been reached and the fruit is soft.

5 Season and ladle into sterilised jars. Seal and label.

Tomato ketchup

If you want to try your hand at making your own tomato ketchup it is certainly worthwhile, but you should not expect it to taste like the commercially bottled varieties.

1kg (2lb 3oz) ripe tomatoes, chopped

2 onions, chopped

115g (4oz) light brown sugar

1 garlic clove, crushed

1 tsp salt

140ml (5fl oz / 1/4 pint) wine vinegar

Optional:
Cloves / cinnamon / cayenne pepper

* Use this recipe to make fruit ketchups by replacing the tomatoes with stoned plums or damsons and adding a few ounces of currants or raisins.

1 Add all the ingredients to a pan and bring to the boil. For a spicier ketchup, add spices or cayenne pepper.

2 Simmer for about 30-40 minutes, stirring frequently to prevent burning. The mixture will become very soft and thick.

3 Sieve, pressing down the mixture to extract all the juices.

4 Return to a clean pan and bring to the boil.

5 Bottle in hot, sterilised, jars. Seal and label.

RELISHES

Relishes, like chutneys, involve the use of vinegar or lemon juice, but they tend to be less thick than chutneys as they are not cooked for nearly so long. You can normally distinguish the main constituents of a relish in the form of chunks or diced pieces. As well as cooked relishes you can also make them with entirely raw ingredients (where they are similar to salsas) and either eat them fresh or bottle them for future use.

Relishes are usually eaten as an accompaniment to savoury dishes such as omelettes, hot or cold meats or smoked fish, or even as a spread.

Relishes won't keep as long as chutneys, but you can bottle them in hot, sterilised jars to increase their shelf life.

Tomato and cucumber relish

Mix together equal quantities of finely chopped tomato, red onion and cucumber, season with salt, sugar and lemon juice and stir in some chopped coriander leaves. You could also add a chopped chilli for extra heat.

Apple relish

Mix together 2 finely chopped eating apples and one finely chopped onion with 2-3 tbsp of wine vinegar, 1 tbsp of olive oil, and some chopped dill.

Beetroot relish

1 cooked beetroot, finely diced, not soaked in vinegar

1/2 red onion, finely chopped

Parsley, chopped

Olive oil

Wholegrain mustard

Lemon juice

1 Mix the beetroot with the red onion and parsley.

2 Add a dressing of olive oil, wholegrain mustard and lemon juice.

Radish relish

450g (1lb) radishes

1 large onion

1 red pepper

140g (5oz) sugar

1 tbsp mustard seeds

1 tbsp dill seeds

2 tsp salt

255ml (9fl oz) vinegar

1 Grate or chop the vegetables.

2 Mix with the rest of the ingredients in a large pan and leave to steep for a couple of hours.

3 Bring to the boil and simmer for 10 minutes.

Plum and onion relish

1 tbsp olive oil

1/2 red onion, chopped

3 plums, stones removed, roughly chopped

2 tbsp brown sugar

1 tbsp clear honey

2 tbsp red wine vinegar

1 lime, juice only

1 Heat the oil in a frying pan.

2 Add the red onion and plums and fry for a few minutes.

3 Add the remaining ingredients, bring to the boil and simmer until soft.

4 Spoon into a small serving bowl and leave to cool.

Relish is a delicious way to use up a glut of plums.

Cucumber and pepper relish

510g (1lb 2oz) cucumber, diced

225g (8oz) onion, diced

55g (2oz) celery, diced

100g (3 1/2 oz) each of red peppers and green peppers, diced

255ml (9fl oz) wine vinegar

140g (5oz) sugar

1/4 tsp celery seeds

1/2 tsp turmeric

1/2 tsp salt

15g (1/2 oz) cornflour

1 Soak the vegetables in salted water for 12 hours and then drain well to draw out the water.

2 Bring the vinegar, sugar, celery seeds, turmeric and salt to the boil.

3 Add the cornflour mixed with a little water and boil for 5 minutes.

4 Add the drained vegetables and boil for 10 minutes.

Rhubarb relish

1 stalk rhubarb, chopped

1 tbsp soft brown sugar

1 tbsp white wine

2 tbsp white wine vinegar

Pinch of chilli powder

Small handful fresh basil, chopped

1 Gently simmer all the ingredients except the herbs for 10-15 minutes until thick.

2 Remove from the heat and stir in the basil.

3 Leave to cool.

SALSAS

Salsas were brought over from Mexico and Central America and are really a modern version of relishes that have now become part of the British diet as an accompaniment to meat and fish dishes. They are commonly based around vegetables such as tomatoes and red peppers, or tropical fruit like mangoes or pineapples, and they always use very fresh ingredients. You can easily invent your own versions by simply combining a main vegetable or fruit with seasonings and finely diced onion or garlic. Pep them up with different herbs or finely chopped chillies, and perhaps a little lime or lemon juice, and serve straight away.

Courgette and tomato salsa

Fry a chopped courgette in olive oil for 4-6 minutes until just turning brown and then season and mix with a couple of finely chopped tomatoes, half an onion and lemon juice.

Tomato and basil salsa

Combine chopped tomatoes, garlic, parsley and basil and season well with salt and pepper.

For the following four salsas, simply combine all the ingredients, season well and chill before serving.

Carrot salsa

3 carrots, peeled and diced
1 tbsp red onion, diced
2 tbsp red and yellow peppers, diced
1 tbsp coriander, fresh, chopped
1 tbsp lemon juice
Salt and pepper
Optional:
1 chilli, finely diced

Cucumber salsa

1 medium cucumber, finely diced
2 tomatoes, chopped
1 red onion, chopped
1/4 red chilli, chopped
1 tbsp mint leaves, chopped
2 tbsp white wine vinegar
1 tsp soy sauce

Raspberry salsa

This works well as a fruity contrast to roast meat.

115g (4oz) fresh raspberries
1/2 red onion, chopped
1/2 garlic clove, crushed
1 tbsp coriander, fresh, chopped
1/2 tsp caster sugar
3 tbsp lemon juice / lime juice
Optional:
1 tsp chilli, finely diced

Pear salsa

3 ripe pears, peeled and chopped
1/2 onion, chopped
1 tsp fresh mint, chopped
1 tsp fresh coriander, chopped
1 tsp sugar
2 tbsp lemon or lime juice
Optional:
1 chilli, finely diced

PICKLES

Pickling is a process used to preserve fruit and vegetables by steeping them in vinegar. It works particularly well with cucumbers, courgettes, marrows, runner beans, onions and beetroot, as well as large fruits such as damsons, plums and pears.

Depending on how strong your vegetables or fruit are, you can use malt, white distilled, cider, red or white wine vinegar.

As you must never add hot liquid to cold jars, sterilise clean glass jars by warming them in a low oven before adding the hot vinegar. Also, make sure the lids are glass or plastic, as vinegar reacts with metal. Ideally, cover with a waxed disc before putting on the lid. When filling the jars, leave a small space at the top after adding the vinegar but always make sure that all the solid contents are completely immersed.

If you can, leave pickled fruit and vegetables several weeks before opening the jars so that they have a chance to absorb all the flavours.

Pickled vegetables

If you want to retain the crispness of certain vegetables, it is best to layer them with salt or soak them in a salt solution the day before and then rinse and dry them thoroughly before carrying out the pickling process.

Raw vegetables in cold spiced vinegar

If you are using vegetables that don't need cooking first, one pickling method is to pack the salted, rinsed and well-dried vegetables in jars and simply cover them with cold, spiced, pickling vinegar. You can also add garlic cloves, whole peppercorns or chilli flakes to the jar for a hotter pickle. Vegetables that would work well with this method include green beans, runner beans, mangetout, sugar snap peas, sliced carrots or radishes.

1 Tie your chosen spices in a muslin bag (see box) and hang this inside a jar full of vinegar.

2 Place the jar in a saucepan half filled with water.

3 Bring the water to the boil and then turn off the heat.

4 Cover the jar and leave the spices to steep in the warm vinegar for 2-3 hours.

5 Discard the spices and then pour the vinegar over your prepared vegetables. Seal and label.

Spices

You can use any mixture of herbs or spices for pickled vegetables, such as whole cinnamon, cloves, coriander, allspice, turmeric, black peppercorns, mustard seed and bay leaves. Conventionally, dill is added to pickled cucumbers.

If you don't want to keep the spices, tie them in a muslin bag so they can be removed easily or strain the vinegar before bottling. You may prefer to leave the spices in the jars, however; they can be eaten and will add decoration.

Hot spiced vinegar

For a sweeter pickle, simmer the vinegar and spices with sugar first to dissolve it and then either cook the vinegar and vegetables together or just add the vegetables at the last minute to heat through. The hot vegetables are then bottled together with the vinegar. This method is best if you want to retain colour, for example when pickling beetroot or cucumbers.

Pickled beetroot

1kg (2lb 3oz) beetroot

710ml (25fl oz) red wine vinegar

1 tsp coriander seeds

1 tsp peppercorns

4 cloves

1 bay leaf

40-55g (1 1/2 -2oz) sugar, to taste

1   Cook the beetroot (quickest in the microwave) and peel when cool.

2   Leave whole or, just before bottling, cut into thick slices.

3   Boil the vinegar with the herbs and spices for about 1 minute and then turn off the heat. Add some sugar if you prefer a sweeter pickle and stir to dissolve.

4   Leave to cool for several hours, so the spices flavour the vinegar.

5   When ready to bottle, heat the vinegar to boiling point, strain first or pour over the beetroot placed in hot, sterilised jars. Seal and label.

Hot piccalilli

1.3kg (3lb) mixed vegetables, diced e.g. courgettes, tomatoes, cucumber, beans and onions (but not root vegetables)

Salt

570ml (20fl oz / 1 pint) white distilled vinegar

85g (3oz) sugar

2 tsp ground turmeric

2 tsp ground ginger

1 tsp dry mustard

15g (1/2 oz) cornflour

1   Layer the vegetables with salt overnight.

2   Rinse thoroughly and dry.

3   Bring the vinegar, sugar and spices to the boil.

4   Add the vegetables and simmer until the vegetables are just cooked but still crisp.

5   Stir in the cornflour blended with a little vinegar and boil for 2-3 minutes.

6   Pack into sterilised jars, seal and label.

Pickled cucumbers

This recipe also works well with courgettes, but you may prefer
to leave out the dill.

3-4 large cucumbers (or 7-8 small ones), sliced

3 onions, sliced

Salt

Spiced vinegar:
570ml (20fl oz / 1 pint) white wine vinegar

450g (1lb) soft brown sugar

1/2 tsp turmeric, ground

1/2 tsp cloves, ground

Dill, fresh

1   Salt the cucumber and sliced onions overnight. Rinse well and then dry.

2   Heat the spiced vinegar ingredients together gently to dissolve the sugar.

3   Add the vegetables to the vinegar and heat to boiling point.

4   Boil for 2-3 minutes, then remove the vegetables and pack into hot, sterilised jars.

5   Continue heating the vinegar for about 10 minutes.

6   Pour the vinegar over the vegetables in the sterilised jars, making sure they are fully submerged and add some dill. Seal and label.

Pickled runner beans

Either use a mixture of turmeric and mustard as recommended by
various celebrity chefs for a piccalilli-like yellow colour or use more
conventional spices such as allspice and peppercorns.

900g (2lb) runner beans, sliced

450g (1lb) onions, chopped

570ml (20fl oz / 1 pint) malt vinegar / wine vinegar

450g (1lb) brown sugar

2 tsp dry mustard

1 tbsp turmeric

Salt

Optional:
1 tbsp cornflour

1   Cook the beans in salted water for about 10 minutes and then drain.

2   Add the onions and vinegar to a large pan.

3   Bring to the boil then simmer for about 10 minutes.

4   Add the sugar and continue simmering until dissolved.

5   Mix the dry spices with a little vinegar to make a paste, add to the pan together with the beans and then simmer for a further 10 minutes. Use cornflour if you want a thicker result.

6   Pack in hot, sterilised, jars. Seal and label.

Pickled fruit

When pickling fruit, you can layer the pieces in salt first or simply heat the fruit with the vinegar, sugar and spices until soft before placing the strained fruit in jars. Recipes for fruit pickles often suggest you remove the spices and then boil the vinegar until it becomes further reduced and syrupy before pouring it over the fruit. This then makes a lovely thick sauce when serving the fruit as a dessert.

As with pickled vegetables, there are a wide range of spices and extra ingredients you can use to flavour your pickles. For example, an attractive combination includes cloves, cinnamon, juniper berries, allspice, ginger and lemon peel.

Pickled plums

1kg (2lb 3oz) plums, washed, dried

285g (10oz) sugar

570ml (20fl oz / 1 pint) red wine vinegar

6 cloves

6-8 whole peppercorns

1 stick cinnamon, broken

1   Dissolve the sugar in the vinegar, add the spices and simmer for 5-10 minutes.

2   Pack the plums in warm, sterilised jars and cover with the hot vinegar.

3   Seal, label and leave for several months.

✳ These go particularly well with smoked meats or cheese.

Pickled blackberries go really well with chicken or game.

Pickled blackberries

As well as pickling whole fruit, you can cook currants and berries with vinegar to make more of a spread that will go well with meat or fish.

450g (1lb) blackberries, washed

200g (7oz) caster sugar

1 tbsp ground spices, e.g. cinnamon, cloves or ginger

285ml (10fl oz / 1/2 pint) white wine vinegar

1 Soak the fruit overnight in a bowl with the sugar and spices.

2 Bring the vinegar to the boil and then add the blackberry mixture.

3 Simmer for 20-30 minutes until the mixture thickens. Do not stir or you will break up the fruit.

4 Pot in hot, sterilised jars, seal and label.

Spiced pickled pears

900g (2lb) firm pears, peeled but still whole with stalk intact (or use quarters)

340g (12oz) soft brown sugar

570ml (20fl oz / 1 pint) cider / white wine vinegar (or mix of cider and white wine vinegar)

Spices, e.g. broken cinnamon sticks, cloves, allspice

Optional: 1 lemon, sliced

1 Simmer the vinegar, sugar and spices until the sugar has fully dissolved.

2 Add the pears and, if using, the lemon slices, and cook gently for 15 minutes or until the fruit is tender.

3 Transfer the drained fruit to warm, sterilised, glass jars using a slotted spoon.

4 Boil the vinegar mixture vigorously for a further 5 minutes or until it has reduced in quantity and started to thicken.

5 Pour the liquid over the fruit and then seal and label the jars.

JAMS

Jam is made in four simple stages:

1 Cook fruit down to a soft pulp. You can use single fruits or a mixture.
2 Add the right amount of sugar and heat gently until the sugar has completely dissolved.
3 Boil the fruit and sugar mixture for several minutes until it reaches setting point.
4 Cool the jam and then pot in sterilised jars.

Recipes using 900g (2lb) fruit will make about 1.3kg (3lb) of jam. If you don't want any seeds in the jam, sieve the cooked fruit before adding the sugar.

Setting your jam

It is the pectin content of fruit that determines how easily it sets.

When making jam with fruit that has a high pectin content, such as black-currants, plums, apples, redcurrants, damsons or gooseberries, you can use ordinary granulated sugar, but the jam will set quicker and with less froth if you use the more expensive preserving sugar, which has larger sugar crystals.

If you use low-pectin fruit, such as strawberries or blackberries, add lemon juice, although you may also need to use special jam sugar containing added pectin. An alternative is to mix in some high-pectin fruit.

To test if jam is set

- Use a sugar thermometer: dip it in hot water and then check that the jam has reached 105°C (220°F).

Or:

- Place several saucers in the freezer. When you are ready to test, turn off the heat, spoon a small amount of jam mixture on to a cold saucer, leave it a few seconds to cool, and then push it gently forwards with your finger. If the jam skin crinkles up rather than remaining smooth and runny, it is set. If not, repeat the boiling and test again every 5 minutes.

Avoiding problems

Unless the fruit is well cooked before any sugar is added, it may not soften, so always give that part of the recipe enough time. If you can, use at least some fruit that is slightly under-ripe as this will contain more pectin. As you won't want to introduce too much water into the recipe which might affect the concentration of sugar, take care when washing the fruit.

The sugar in the mixture must be dissolved before you start boiling. To help it dissolve easily, warm it in the oven before adding it to the fruit and then check by coating the back of a wooden spoon with the mixture. If it has dissolved properly, no sugar crystals will be visible.

As you need to boil jam fairly vigorously, it is very important to use a large enough pan such as a proper maslin or preserving pan. This will allow you to boil the mixture rapidly without the risk of it boiling over the top and on to the stove.

Scum often develops on the top of jams and jellies as they are being heated, which doesn't look very nice. To disperse it you can add a small knob of butter to the pan or sterilise a metal spoon in hot water and then use it to gently push the scum to the edge of the pan where it can be easily removed.

Potting your jam

To sterilise jam jars, make sure you thoroughly wash them out and then heat them in a low oven for half an hour before use.

You should make sure that the jam jars are still hot when potting up, as this will stop them cracking when you pour in the hot jam.

Cover the surface of the jam with waxed discs straight away and then add cellophane held with elastic bands, or jar lids. It is quite safe to wait 10-15 minutes from pouring in the jam to do this. Waiting is necessary before potting jam containing whole fruit if you want the pieces to spread throughout the jar as otherwise they will rise to the surface.

Always label your jam with the fruit mixture and date. Labels will easily drop off hot jars, so add labels when the jam has cooled.

You can buy cheap jam kits from many general stores that contain discs and cellophane as well as labels. If you buy just one specialist piece of jam-making equipment, I suggest you make it a jam funnel. This useful little device made of plastic or stainless steel only costs a few pounds and makes ladling or pouring your jam into jars without any spills a very easy task.

There is really nothing like home-made jam and bread.

Blackcurrant jam

900g (2lb) blackcurrants

570ml (20fl oz / 1 pint) water

1.1kg (2lb 8oz) sugar

1 Pick over the fruit to remove stalks and leaves and then place in a large saucepan.

2 Add the water and simmer for 30 minutes or until soft.

3 Add the sugar and continue cooking until it has dissolved.

4 Now boil rapidly and keep boiling for 10 minutes, or until setting point is reached.

5 When setting point is reached, cool for 15 minutes and then ladle into hot, sterilised jars, seal and label.

Blackberry (and apple) jam

13kg (3lb) blackberries

900g (2lb) jam sugar

1 tbsp lemon juice

Optional:

Replace up to half the fruit with chopped cooking apples – and then use granulated sugar in place of jam sugar

1 Clean the fruit and simmer with the lemon juice until soft, adding a little water only if necessary.

2 Sieve the fruit if you don't like the seeds.

3 Stir in the sugar and simmer until it has dissolved.

4 Boil rapidly for 10 minutes or until setting point is reached.

5 Pour into hot, sterilised jars, seal and label.

Raspberry jam

1kg (2lb 3oz) raspberries

1kg (2lb 3oz) sugar

3 tbsp lemon juice

Optional:
Replace some of the raspberries with redcurrants, which have a high pectin content

1   Check over and hull the raspberries.
2   Cook without added water until soft and then sieve if you prefer to make seedless jam.
3   Stir in the sugar and lemon juice and simmer until all the sugar has dissolved.
4   Boil for 10 minutes or until setting point is reached.
5   Pour into hot, sterilised jars, seal and label.

Gooseberry jam

900g (2lb) fruit, topped and tailed

900g (2lb) granulated sugar

570ml (20fl oz / 1 pint) water

1   Cook the fruit in water until soft.
2   Add the sugar and warm gently to dissolve.
3   Boil for 10 minutes or until setting point is reached.
4   Pour into hot, sterilised jars, seal and label.

Plum jam

When using stoned fruit for jam, you can either stone it first (use a cherry stoner for small fruit) or lift out the stones with a slotted spoon as the fruit is stewing. The former method may be better as you need to take care that you remove all the stones; someone breaking their tooth on their toast and jam will not thank you.

900g (2lb) fruit, stoned (chop up large fruits for quicker cooking)

225ml (8fl oz) water

680g (1lb 8oz) sugar

(For damsons, use 1kg [2lb 3oz] sugar and 425ml [15fl oz / 3/4 pint] water with 1.3kg [3lb] fruit.)

1   Simmer the fruit in the water until it is soft.
2   Add the sugar and dissolve thoroughly.
3   Boil for 10 minutes or until setting point is reached.
4   Pour into hot, sterilised jars, seal and label.

Strawberry jam

900g (2lb) strawberries, hulled

790g (1lb 12oz) sugar

3 tbsp lemon juice

1. Combine the fruit with the sugar in a large pan. (If you have time, layer the fruit with the sugar and leave overnight. The sugar will dissolve, drawing out the juices and firming up the fruit at the same time.)
2. Warm the pan to soften the fruit. Make sure all the sugar has dissolved.
3. Add the lemon juice.
4. Bring the pan to the boil and boil rapidly for 10 minutes or until setting point is reached.
5. Allow the jam to settle for 15 minutes or the fruit will rise to the top, and then pour into hot, sterilised jars, seal and label.

JELLIES

These can be made with any fruit, including apples, plums, currants or berries. They differ from jam as they contain only juice, and so they are a particularly good way to deal with fruit like raspberries and blackberries that have lots of seeds.

It is easiest to make jellies if you have a jelly or muslin bag. After cooking the fruit until it is soft, tie the bag over the mouth of a large jug or suspend it over a container, then spoon or pour in the cooked fruit. Let it strain through for several hours and don't be tempted to squeeze out the last drops or this will make the jelly cloudy.

The resultant juice is then mixed with sugar in the proportion 450g (1lb) sugar to 570ml (20fl oz / 1 pint) liquid, heated to dissolve the sugar and then boiled until setting point is reached.

Apple jelly

300g (10 1/2 oz) cooking apples

200ml (7fl oz) water

Sugar – 450g (1lb) to 570ml (20fl oz / 1 pint) juice

You will also need:

Muslin / jelly bag

1. Wash, chop up and then cook the apples in the water until soft.
2. Strain the juice through a muslin or jelly bag.
3. Measure the juice and add the right amount of sugar, then return to the pan.
4. Warm to dissolve the sugar and then boil until setting point is reached.
5. Bottle in hot, sterilised jars, seal and label.

* If you add herbs such as rosemary to the jelly, it makes an unusual savoury accompaniment to pork or ham.

Redcurrant jelly

1kg (2lb 3oz) redcurrants

570ml (20fl oz / 1 pint) water

Sugar – 450g (1lb) to 570ml (20fl oz / 1 pint) juice

You will also need:

Muslin / jelly bag

1. Wash the currants and pick out any leaves. There is no need to strip the stalks.
2. Place in a pan with the water and cook until soft (10-15 minutes). Mash down the fruit now and again with a wooden spoon to extract all the juice.
3. Pour into a muslin bag and strain over a bowl for several hours.
4. Measure the extract and mix with the right amount of sugar.
5. Warm the mixture to dissolve the sugar and then bring to the boil. Boil rapidly for 5-10 minutes until setting point is reached.
6. Bottle in hot, sterilised jars, seal and label.

FRUIT CHEESES AND BUTTERS

Fruit cheeses are firm, jelly-like preserves, made by heating fruit purée with sugar long enough to form a thick paste. They are a good way to use up the pulp left over from making jellies, and can be set in a mould and cut into slices, then kept in the fridge or sugar-coated and stored in an airtight tin. Fruits that stew down into a thick pulp, such as apples, plums, damsons or pears, are ideal, but you can also use berries and currants. Fruit butters are similar but contain less sugar, so are spreadable but do not keep so long. As a general rule of thumb, cheeses are made using 450g (1lb) sugar for every 570ml (20fl oz / 1 pint) of purée, or an equal weight of sugar to pulp; butters use 340g (12oz) sugar for every 570ml (20fl oz / 1 pint) or 450g (1lb) of purée.

Damson cheese

680g (1lb 8oz) damsons

100ml (3 1/2 fl oz) water

Sugar – equal weight of sugar to pulp or 450g (1lb) sugar to 570ml (20fl oz / 1 pint) pulp

1   Stew the damsons in the water for 20-30 minutes.

2   Sieve the fruit, pressing down to extract all the juice.

3   Return the pulp to a clean pan with the sugar. Warm gently to dissolve all the sugar.

4   Continue boiling for up to 40-60 minutes until it is very thick. Keep stirring during cooking to make sure it doesn't burn.

5   Pot like jam in sterilised jars or spoon into a greased mould or shallow baking tin lined with non-stick baking paper and leave to cool.

Redcurrant cheese

450g (1lb) redcurrants

285ml (10fl oz / 1/2 pint) water

Sugar – equal weight of sugar to pulp or 450g (1lb) sugar to 570ml (20fl oz / 1 pint) pulp

1   Use the pulp left over from making jelly mixed with a little hot water or cook fresh redcurrants until soft Sieve out the pips.

2   Gently heat the pulp with the sugar until the sugar has dissolved.

3   Simmer until the mixture is very thick, stirring frequently. Take care that it doesn't burn, as it could take up to an hour.

4   Pot in sterilised jars or spoon into a greased mould or shallow baking tin, as for damson cheese above.

Apple and plum butter

900g (2lb) apples, chopped

450g (1lb) plums, pitted

Sugar – 340g (12oz) for every 570ml (20fl oz / 1 pint) fruit purée

Optional:

Butter

1 Cook the fruit in a little water until soft.

2 Sieve and then add the correct proportion of sugar.

3 Return to the pan, heat to dissolve the sugar and then cook gently for 20-30 minutes until thick and creamy. Stir regularly to prevent burning.

4 You can add a little butter for a glossy finish.

5 Pot in hot, sterilised, jars, seal and label.

MINCEMEAT

Everyone has their favourite recipe for mincemeat, but here is one that seems to work very well.

Makes enough to fill 3-4 450g (1lb) jars

450g (1lb) cooking apples / green apples, grated / finely chopped

115g (4oz) shredded suet

225g (8oz) brown sugar

565g (1lb 4oz) mixed raisins, sultanas and currants

115g (4oz) chopped candied peel and/or glacé cherries

115g (4oz) chopped nuts, e.g. almonds

1 tbsp mixed spice

1/2 tsp nutmeg, ground

1/2 tsp cinnamon, ground

2 tsp orange zest and/or lemon zest

2 tbsp orange juice

2 tbsp lemon juice

4 tbsp brandy

1 Mix all the ingredients except the brandy together.

2 If you have time, cover and leave to mature for a day, stirring regularly.

3 To help your mincemeat keep longer, warm the mixture on the hob or in a very low oven (120°C / 250°F / Gas Mark 1/2) for 2-3 hours. Stir well and you will coat the ingredients with warm suet and help prevent the juices in the fruit from running out and fermenting. (The end result will look a little grey in the jar but it should keep much better than otherwise.)

4 Stir in the brandy and pot into sterilised jars, pushing the mixture down firmly and tapping to remove all air bubbles. Seal and label.

* If your mincemeat seems too dry, just add extra brandy.

VEGETABLE PRESERVES

Some jams and other preserves can be made with vegetables, and
you can use them to accompany both savoury and sweet dishes.

Squash butter

3 medium squash, halved
(roughly 1.3kg [3lb] weight),
de-seeded

115ml (4fl oz) apple juice

170g (6oz) brown sugar

1 tsp mixed spices, e.g. ground
ginger, cinnamon and nutmeg

1. Bake the squash at 180°C (360°F / Gas Mark 4) for about 1 hour until soft. Scoop out the flesh. Blend if you want a very smooth butter.

2. Mix the purée in a saucepan with the rest of the ingredients.

3. Warm gently to dissolve the sugar and then replace the lid and continue simmering for 30-40 minutes until the mixture is thick and spreadable. Stir regularly to prevent burning.

4. Pot in sterilised jars, seal and label, or store in airtight containers in the fridge.

Tomato marmalade

This is a very nice complement to breakfast
bacon, sausage and eggs.

1kg (2lb 3oz) tomatoes,
firm, ripe

Sugar – equal weight
of sugar to pulp or 450g (1lb)
sugar to 570ml (20fl oz /
1 pint) pulp

Spices, e.g. cloves, cinnamon
stick

100ml (3 1/2 fl oz) water

3 tbsp lemon juice (or include
grated zest of 1 unwaxed
lemon)

1. Simmer the tomatoes and spices in water for 20 minutes.

2. Sieve the pulp and add the sugar.

3. Return the pulp to the pan and warm gently until the sugar has dissolved.

4. Add the lemon juice, bring to the boil and boil for about 10 minutes until setting point is reached.

5. Pot in sterilised jars, seal and label.

Both marrows and rhubarb go well with ginger to make jam.

Marrow and ginger jam

I have tried, and failed, to make jam with courgettes: the flavour is too light to be worthwhile. Either use mature marrows or replace half the quantity of vegetable with fruit such as damsons or plums.

1.3kg (3lb) marrows / marrows mixed with damsons or plums

55g (2oz) ginger root, bruised / chopped into large pieces

4 tbsp lemon juice

1.3kg (3lb) sugar

Optional: 450g (1lb) cooking apples, peeled

You will also need:
Muslin

> ✳ You can use exactly the same quantities to make rhubarb and ginger jam. To make sure the sugar dissolves, add it to the chopped rhubarb stalks and leave to soak overnight.

1   Peel, de-seed and cube the marrows and stone and chop other fruit.

2   Core and chop the apples, if using. (They will help the jam set.)

3   Simmer the marrows, damsons and apple with lemon juice until soft enough to mash.

4   Tie the ginger in muslin and hang in the preserving pan.

5   Add the sugar and simmer until the sugar dissolves.

6   Now cook for 20-30 minutes until setting point is reached. This takes longer than fruit jam, but take care it doesn't dry out or burn.

7   Pot the jam in sterilised jars, seal and label.

8   If you can, leave it to mature for a few months before using.

CANDIED FRUIT

If you want to do something a little different with plums, apples or pears and have some time on your hands, you can create candied fruit. This works by replacing the water in the fruit with sugar.

You need to take unblemished fruit and, after blanching to break down the fibres, soak it in increasingly strong sugar solutions until you have pastel-coloured, transparent-looking glacé fruit sweets. They are usually served dusted with icing sugar – just like Turkish delight – and make excellent presents.

510g (1lb 2oz) fruit, washed, peeled and stoned

680g (1lb 8oz) caster sugar

285ml (10fl oz / 1/2 pint) water

1   Leave small fruit such as Mirabelle plums whole but chop larger fruit such as apples, Victoria plums or pears in half, quarters or slices or any suitable size for eating.

2   Blanch the fruit by cooking in boiling water for 30 seconds and then transferring to a bowl of cold water.

3   Make the first syrup solution by dissolving 255g (9oz) of sugar in the water and bringing this to the boil. Simmer for 2-3 minutes.

4   Off the heat, pour the syrup over the pieces of fruit and make sure they are completely covered.

5   Leave for 24 hours.

6   Lift out the fruit and increase the strength of the solution. Do this by adding a further 55g (2oz) sugar, bring to the boil and boil for 1-2 minutes.

7   Pour the syrup over the fruit and leave for a further 24 hours.

8   Repeat over the next 3 days, adding another 55g (2oz) sugar to the syrup and boiling for 1 minute each time. The syrup will become increasingly thick when it is cooled.

9   On Day 6, add 100g (3.5oz) sugar to the solution, bring to the boil and this time add the fruit and simmer for 2-3 minutes.

10 Remove from the heat and leave for 48 hours.

11 On Day 8, repeat with a further 100g (3.5oz) sugar and 2-3 minutes' simmering before leaving the fruit to soak for a final 48 hours.

12 Either store the finished fruit in the syrup or drain the fruit using a sieve and place on a rack to dry completely.

13 Store dried candied fruit in an airtight container away from light and moisture.

> ✳ For pure indulgence, dip your candied fruit in melted chocolate.

Chapter 9
Bottled fruit and vegetables

BOTTLING TECHNIQUES

BOTTLED FRUIT

BOTTLED VEGETABLES

BOTTLING TECHNIQUES

There is nothing like a shelf of gleaming jars of golden plums or mixed berries, and it is reasonably easy to bottle your own produce in the kitchen. Jars must be sterilised carefully before being used.

Sterilising the containers

Some people sterilise jars in the dishwasher, but I prefer to use the oven. Before use, wash the jars in warm soapy water, rinse and dry and then put them on baking trays. Heat them in the oven at 150°C (300°F / Gas Mark 2) for at least 15 minutes and keep them hot so they will take any hot liquid without cracking. The jars can be re-used, but replace the rubber seals each year, as they will perish. You also need to sterilise the lids and clips for bottled produce, which can be done by boiling them in water for 10 minutes.

For produce to store in the fridge and use up within a few weeks, the two bottling methods that do not require special equipment are a hot water bath or the oven.

Take particular care when bottling produce

The one issue that needs to be addressed when bottling, particularly when using low-acid vegetables, is food poisoning. If the jars and their contents are not sterilised, heated to a high temperature and packed under vacuum to exclude all air, it is possible that they will become contaminated. The reason this is a particular issue when bottling, as opposed to potting up jams, chutneys and pickles, is that bottled preserves don't contain large enough amounts of sugar, alcohol or vinegar to act as a preservative.

A vacuum is created as the contents cool and so it is very important to bottle hot and to test the seal of the bottle or jar. Different bottling methods include heating the jars in a boiling water bath or under pressure, and these are considered the safest methods if you want to store your bottled produce outside the fridge for any length of time. If you decide you want to bottle vegetables such as carrots or beans, the only real answer is to buy a professional pressure canner/bottler.

Bottling using the hot water method

- Clean and sterilise jars and fill with cooked fruit and hot liquor as described in the recipes.
- Try to release any air, for example by tapping the jars or inserting a skewer, and then seal the jars but do not over-tighten the lids.
- Place in a pan of warm water to completely cover the jars, making sure they do not touch one another or the sides or bottom of the container in case they crack. One way is to separate them with cardboard or wads of newspaper and to stand them on a wire rack.
- Bring the water slowly to a rolling boil and boil for 10-30 minutes to make sure the heat penetrates into the centre of each jar. Pickles take the shortest time and fresh fruit the longest. Tomatoes may need up to 1 hour.
- Lift the jars out with tongs and place on absorbent paper. Seal tightly and leave for 24 hours before testing the seal (see right).

✳ You can preserve fruit in some alcohols such as vodka, brandy or rum without special treatment as bacteria cannot grow in them, but if using wine or cider, the jars will still need to be heated.

Bottling using the oven

The recipes give full details, but in general terms:

- Set the oven at 150°C (300°F / Gas Mark 2).
- Use jars with special clips or screw-on lids and a rubber seal. The two most well-known manufacturers of these jars are Kilner and Le Parfait.
- Although jars should be well filled before going into the oven, tap them to release any air and leave a small gap at the top for expansion before putting on the lid.
- Do not over-tighten the lids at this stage.
- Heat 500ml (18fl oz) jars for 30-40 minutes and 1l (35fl oz / 1 3/4 pint) jars for about 1 hour.
- Once heated, remove jars from the oven with oven gloves and seal the lids tightly.
- Always test the seal (see below) after 24 hours.

Testing the seal

To test the seal of bottled preserves, leave the jars to cool for 24 hours and then loosen the clips or screws. Holding the rim of the lid, carefully lift up the jar and it should remain attached. If sealed properly, replace the clips straight away; wipe the jars, label and store. If not secure, keep in the fridge and use within a few days.

BOTTLED FRUIT

If you decide you want to bottle your fruit as an alternative to making jam or fruit purée, remember that the whole process will take some time, as you must make sure all bacteria are killed. Fruit you want to bottle should be in excellent condition and certainly not over-ripe.

Bottled pears

1kg (2lb 3oz) pears

115g (4oz) granulated sugar

570ml (20fl oz / 1 pint) water

Few pieces of orange peel

Pieces of cinnamon stick

2-3 cloves

Optional:
Replace half the water with red wine

Lemon juice

1 Peel and then either halve and core the pears or leave whole but with the stalks intact. You can toss them in lemon juice to stop them going brown.

2 Heat the water and sugar with the cloves, cinnamon and orange peel until the sugar has dissolved. For a lovely pink colour, replace half the water with red wine.

3 For the pear pieces, poach them gently for 15 minutes until tender, before bottling in hot jars.

4 For whole pears, bottle the prepared fruit straight away, boil the syrup for 5 minutes and pour into the hot jars to cover the fruit completely.

5 Replace the rubber seals and lids but do not screw up tightly.

6 Return the jars to the oven, spaced out in a roasting tin, and pour in about 2.5cm (1") boiling water or line the tin with newspaper to catch any spills.

7 For poached pears, continue to heat at 150°C (300°F / Gas Mark 2) for the appropriate time depending on the size of the jars.

8 For uncooked pears, heat for a further 30 minutes or so to make sure the fruit is tender.

9 Carefully remove the hot jars from the oven and seal immediately.

10 Cool for 24 hours then test the seal and label.

Plums in brandy

If using small plums in this recipe then they will tend to lose their shape – but will still make for a delicious sauce.

450g (1lb) ripe plums/damsons, pitted and halved

170-255g (6-9oz) granulated sugar

140ml (5fl oz / 1/4 pint) water

Cloves / pieces of cinnamon stick

140ml (5fl oz / 1/4 pint) brandy

1   Heat the sugar in the water until it has dissolved.

2   Bring to the boil and then simmer for 10 minutes.

3   Add the plums and spices to the syrup and poach very gently until just tender.

4   Use a slotted spoon to lift out the fruit and pack in hot, sterilised jars.

5   Boil the syrup for 3-4 minutes.

6   Cool for a few minutes so you don't boil off the alcohol and then add the brandy. If you prefer, fish out the spices at this stage.

7   Pour immediately on to the plums to cover the fruit completely.

8   Tap the jars to release any air, seal tightly and label.

Summer berry preserve

1.3kg (3lb) mixed fruit, e.g. redcurrants, raspberries and blackcurrants

225g (8oz) granulated sugar

570ml (20fl oz / 1 pint) water

115ml (4fl oz) liqueur, e.g. Kirsch

1   Preheat the oven to 120°C (250°F / Gas Mark 1/2).

2   Prepare the fruit – wash, stalk and remove the leaves. Pack into sterilised jars and cover but do not seal tightly.

3   Heat in the oven for 1 hour, when the juices will have started to run.

4   Dissolve the sugar in the water and boil for 5 minutes. Remove from the heat, cool for a few minutes and then stir in the Kirsch.

5   Pour in the hot syrup to completely cover the fruit and tap to make sure there are no trapped air bubbles. Seal, label and store.

BOTTLED VEGETABLES

The vegetables you are most likely to want to bottle under vacuum are tomatoes. You can also store lightly cooked vegetables, such as courgettes, in vinegar and oil for a short time in the fridge, but add lemon juice or vinegar if you want to keep them for longer than a few days. You can add extra nuts and herbs to the jars and try flavoured or nut oils.

Bottled tomatoes (passata)

900g (2lb) tomatoes

1 tbsp lemon juice

Salt to taste

Optional:
Herbs, e.g. basil

You will also need:
Blender

1. Blanch the tomatoes by boiling for a minute or two and then plunging into cold water before removing the skins. You could also remove the core and even scoop out the seeds, but this is a matter of taste.

2. Purée the tomatoes and any herbs in a blender and then pour the mixture into a saucepan.

3. Add the lemon juice and salt to taste and bring to the boil. Simmer gently for 30 minutes or until thick.

4. Pot into sterilised jars, cover and bottle using a water bath or heat in the oven for an appropriate time for the size of jar (see page 212).

5. Seal tightly, cool for 24 hours and then test the seal.

6. Store in the fridge and use up within a few weeks.

Bottled courgettes

1kg (2lb 3oz) courgettes, sliced thickly

2 garlic cloves, chopped

570ml (20fl oz / 1 pint) white wine

500ml (18fl oz) wine vinegar

7g (1/4 oz) salt

Olive oil / walnut-flavoured oil / hazelnut-flavoured oil

Herbs, e.g. chopped parsley or thyme

Optional: Nuts

1. Bring the wine, vinegar and salt to the boil, add the courgettes and cook for 2-3 minutes.

2. Drain the vegetables and combine with the garlic, nuts (if using) and herbs in hot, sterilised, jars.

3. Cover completely with oil, tapping the jars to remove any air, and seal straight away.

4. Store in the fridge and keep for only a few days. Once opened, add extra oil to make sure the vegetables are always covered.

Chapter 10
Dried fruit and vegetables

DRIED FRUIT AND FRUIT LEATHERS

DRIED VEGETABLES

DRIED FRUIT AND FRUIT LEATHERS

As a healthy alternative to fresh fruit, it is very easy to dry your own apple, pear or plum slices. You can substitute dried fruit for fresh in your cooking, although you may need to soak it for a few hours first. Use ripe, undamaged fruit for drying, and peel any tough-skinned ones. If you are keeping the skins on, pierce them to let out moisture. The pieces should not touch each other as they dry.

You can use a normal domestic oven for drying, but it needs to be set at a very low temperature (around 60-110°C / 140-230°F / Gas Mark 0- 1/4) and the door may need to be propped open to ensure that the moisture in the fruit is removed. You could also try drying in a warm room or an airing cupboard (again, with plentiful ventilation) or outside on a hot day – although in the UK this could take 3-4 days.

Leathering is the process used for drying puréed fruit, so is ideal if your produce is no longer looking its best. The purée is spread out in a layer on a tray and then dried in the oven. When it is completely dry, you can cut leathers into strips that roll up – just like beef jerky.

Dried apple rings

You can dry both eating and cooking apples, but cooking apples will be chewier and less likely to go brittle.

1   Peel and core the apples, removing any sign of a blemish. (If you don't have an apple corer, slice the fruit first and then cut out the centre, or for large numbers of apples, forget rings and just cut slices.)

2   Slice thinly – 0.5cm (1/4") – unless you want chunkier, chewy pieces.

3   Rinse in water with a little lemon juice to prevent discolouring, but don't overdo the lemon or it will taint the taste.

4   *To dry:* spread the rings out in the sun on paper, turning regularly, or hang them up threaded on garden canes, outdoors or in a warm or sunny room.

Or: Place the rings directly on greased oven racks or thread them on canes that can rest on the edges of a baking tray and dry in the oven at a low temperature for 4-6 hours.

5   Leave to cool and then store in airtight containers. Take care if storing in plastic bags as the fruit can go mouldy.

Home-dried fruit looks and tastes far better than dried fruit in the shops.

Dried plums, pears and damsons

1 Wash and dry the fruit.

2 Cut large fruit in half, quarters or slices and stone or core and pip.

3 Dry on trays or greased racks in the oven at a low temperature for 3-5 hours, or outside on a sunny day. For fruit halves, lay with the cut-side uppermost so that the juice doesn't run out.

4 Store as for apple rings (see page 219).

Cooked fruit leathers

1 Peel, core and chop fresh fruit such as plums, berries, apples or pears, or a mix of fruit.

2 Place the pieces in a saucepan.

3 For very sour fruit, add sugar or honey to the pan – however, drying tends to concentrate the sweetness of most fruit so you shouldn't need much.

4 Simmer for about 10-20 minutes until soft. There should be just enough liquid to prevent burning, so add a little water or apple juice if the fruit seems in danger of drying out.

5 Halfway through the cooking, add some lemon juice to keep the fruit's colour and, as an optional extra, spices such as cinnamon, ground cloves or nutmeg.

6 When the fruit is well cooked, mash it into a thick purée and sieve out any unwanted bits.

7 For very smooth leathers, finish off the purée by liquidising in a blender.

8 Grease a baking tin or line with cling film or other non-stick material that can be used in a low-temperature oven and spread the purée out in a layer 0.25-0.5cm (1/8-1/4") thick.

9 Dry very slowly in a cool oven (50-60°C / 120-140°F) overnight or for 6-8 hours.

10 When it is no longer sticky on top, the leather is ready. Peel it off the lining, cut into strips and roll up. Store in plastic bags in the fridge or freezer.

11 You could also cut small shapes out of a sheet of fruit leather to use as cake or pudding decorations.

DRIED VEGETABLES

The most well-known dried 'vegetable' is the tomato, and oven-dried tomatoes make a very welcome addition to the larder. You can also dry blanched beans or root vegetables such as carrots or beetroot, which can then be kept and added to soups and stews. For root vegetables, peel and slice and then follow the basic fruit drying recipe.

Dried tomatoes

In the UK it is difficult to make truly sun-dried tomatoes, but oven-drying will still provide you with tasty tomatoes that you can keep for months and use in bread, pizzas and sauces.

1 If you want to remove the skins, plunge firm, ripe tomatoes into boiling water and leave for a minute before moving to a bowl of iced water. The skins should slide off easily.

2 Cut into halves or quarters and remove any blemishes. You can also scoop out the seeds.

3 Spread the tomatoes out on racks supported over baking trays, cut-side up, and dry for 8 hours or so in a cool oven (or semi-dry them for 3-4 hours if you are going to keep them in oil). If you like, first sprinkle with dried herbs, sugar, olive oil and a little coarse salt.

4 They are done when they are leathery and a deep red. To ensure that you do not over-dry them and make them too tough to use, check them at regular intervals.

5 Leave them to cool and then either store covered in olive oil containing extra flavourings (such as garlic cloves and herbs) in sterilised jars or in airtight plastic bags in the freezer.

6 Tomatoes in oil-filled jars can keep for several weeks in the fridge, but you must keep them submerged at all times or they will go mouldy.

Chapter 11
Sauces and spreads

SAUCES, PURÉES AND DIPS

COULIS

FRUIT VINEGARS

SAUCES, PURÉES AND DIPS

Excess fruit or vegetables can be turned into sauces for both savoury and sweet dishes, or you can create tasty light lunches or snacks.

The various terms used in this section, such as 'sauces', 'purées', 'dips' and 'spreads', can seem difficult to distinguish – a sauce recipe, for example, can include puréed vegetables or fruit; it may be thin enough to pour, or thick enough to spoon out. As a general rule, a sauce is made with several ingredients that are simmered together to produce a pourable or spoonable liquid. Purées and spreads are usually more substantial and are made up of concentrated or liquid-ised vegetables or fruit. They may need to be chilled before being served, either as a side dish or spread on toast or sliced pitta bread.

If purées or finely diced mixtures of fruit and vegetables are thinned with additions such as cream, yoghurt or cream cheese, they can be served as a dip with carrot sticks, celery, bread or crisps.

As a general rule, 450g (1lb) of fruit or vegetables will make enough purée or sauce for 4 portions.

Spinach pesto

Although pesto is normally made with basil, this is even better as it tastes so fresh and is a wonderful way to eat spinach. The sauce can be stirred into pasta, spread over meat or fish before baking, or mixed with mayonnaise as an unusual salad dressing.

225g (8oz) spinach leaves, torn, washed, stems removed

2 garlic cloves

3 tbsp pine nuts

115g (4oz) Parmesan cheese, grated

1/2 tsp dry basil / handful of fresh leaves

Pinch of salt

Olive oil

You will also need: Blender

1 Place the spinach, garlic, pine nuts, cheese, salt and basil in a blender.

2 Slowly liquidise, adding olive oil until you have a thick paste.

Cranberry, apple and pear sauce

225g (8oz) cranberries, fresh/frozen

1 apple, chopped

2 ripe pears, chopped

1 tsp orange rind, grated

1 tsp cinnamon

140ml (5fl oz / 1/4 pint) orange juice

55g (2oz) sugar, to taste

To serve: Cheese / cold meats

1 Combine all the ingredients in a saucepan.

2 Bring to the boil and then simmer for 10 minutes until the cranberries start to pop and the mixture thickens.

3 Add more sugar if necessary.

4 Serve with cheese or cold meats.

Cucumber and tarragon sauce

1 cucumber, peeled, de-seeded, diced

285ml (10fl oz / 1/2 pint) double cream

3 tsp white wine vinegar

1 tbsp fresh tarragon, chopped

Salt and pepper

1/2 tsp sugar

Icing sugar

To serve: Smoked fish / meat

1 Marinate the cucumber for 30 minutes in 1 tsp vinegar, 1/2 tsp salt and 1/2 tsp sugar.

2 Drain and dry very thoroughly on kitchen paper.

3 Whip the cream and stir in the rest of the vinegar, chopped herbs and a little icing sugar to taste.

4 Stir in the cucumber, season to taste and serve with smoked fish or meat.

Gooseberry sauce

Stew gooseberries in a little water with added butter until soft. Mash in the pan with some cream and sugar or honey to taste. Season with salt and pepper if using with meat or fish.

Plum sauce

This recipe is very rich and goes well with meat or fish and especially with Chinese duck and pancakes.

225g (8oz) plums, stoned and diced

1 onion, diced

1 tbsp olive oil

50g (1.75oz) sugar, e.g. light brown or demerara

140ml (5fl oz / 1/4 pint) vegetable stock / chicken stock

55ml (2fl oz) red wine

1. Gently fry the onion in the oil for 5 minutes, until soft.
2. Add the rest of the ingredients and heat gently to dissolve the sugar.
3. Cook on a medium-high flame for about 5-10 minutes until the sauce is thick and a dark colour.

Tomato sauce

2 tbsp olive oil

1 onion, chopped

1 garlic clove, crushed

450g (1lb) tomatoes, roughly chopped

Handful of chopped fresh basil / oregano

2-3 bay leaves

1/4 glass red wine / water

To season: Salt and pepper

Optional: 1 tsp tomato purée

1. Gently fry the onion and garlic in olive oil until soft and transparent.
2. For a thicker sauce, add the tomato purée and cook for a further minute.
3. Add the tomatoes, bay leaves, basil or oregano and a little red wine or water. Blanch the tomatoes and plunge into cold water first if you want to remove the skins.
4. Season to taste.
5. Simmer for 20-30 minutes until the sauce is thick, adding further liquid if there is a danger that it will dry out.
6. Sieve the sauce for a smoother finish.

Apple purée

Despite using cooking apples, I don't find this dish needs any additional sugar. You will see recipes that add not only sugar but butter, lemon zest and/or cinnamon, but I would suggest you try this simple method first and then jazz it up if you think it really needs additions.

1   Peel and chop several cooking apples and place them in a microwave bowl.

2   Put on a lid, microwave on full power for 3-4 minutes until soft and then gently mash with a fork.

3   If making this on the hob, put apples and a little water in a pan and simmer gently for 10-15 minutes.

Courgette purée

This is excellent as an addition to soups and stews.

450g (1lb) courgettes, sliced

Butter or oil

You will also need:
Blender

1   Sauté sliced courgettes in the butter or oil for a few minutes.

2   Cover the pan and cook until soft. This dish does not need added water but take care it doesn't burn.

3   Liquidise and freeze in suitably small containers.

Beetroot purée

This not only looks fantastic but brings a real zing to cold meats.

450g (1lb) beetroot

1/2 whole chilli, chopped
(or more if you like it hot)

Fresh coriander

1 garlic clove, peeled

2 tbsp balsamic / red wine vinegar

2 tbsp olive oil

115ml (4fl oz) sour cream / plain yoghurt

You will also need:
Blender

To season: Salt and pepper

1   Cook the beetroot – either roast in foil for an hour or microwave with a little water for 5-10 minutes.

2   When cool, peel the beetroot by rubbing off the skin.

3   Liquidise with the rest of the ingredients and season to taste.

Broad bean purée

450g (1lb) broad beans

Lemon juice

Salt and pepper

115g (4oz) mascarpone cheese

Herbs, e.g. savory or thyme

You will also need: Blender

1. Simmer podded broad beans for 5 minutes and, if old, remove the skins.
2. Liquidise with lemon juice, salt and pepper.
3. Add the mascarpone cheese, to thicken.
4. Stir in chopped herbs such as savory or thyme.

* Serve with toast for a delicious snack.

Pea purée

This is an unusual side vegetable dish.

450g (1lb) peas, fresh

570ml (20fl oz / 1 pint) water

Fresh mint

Salt

Optional:
Crème fraiche

You will also need:
Blender

1. Cook the peas in the water.
2. Stir in the mint.
3. Drain but retain the cooking water and liquidise the peas and mint in a blender.
4. For a very smooth purée, sieve as well and add some of the cooking liquid if the purée is too thick. You could also stir in a little crème fraiche.
5. Season and warm through before serving.

Roasted tomato purée

Tomatoes, chopped

Balsamic vinegar

Salt and pepper

Olive oil

Optional:
Garlic cloves

Herbs, e.g. basil

You will also need: Blender

1. Fill an oiled baking dish with tomato and add garlic if you want to include the flavour in your purée.
2. Scatter over salt, pepper, any herbs and a few teaspoons of vinegar.
3. Drizzle over olive oil and then bake until the tomatoes are completely soft.
4. Liquidise in a blender, sieve and then pot in hot, sterilised, jars.

Tomato purée

1kg (2lb 3oz) tomatoes, chopped roughly

1 tsp salt

2 tbsp red wine vinegar

1   Add the tomatoes to a pan with the salt and vinegar.

2   Heat gently until thick and concentrated, adding a little water to prevent the purée burning.

3   Sieve and then bottle in hot, sterilised, jars.

Cucumber and yoghurt dip

This basic recipe goes well with curries and filled pitta, but you can add garlic, lemon juice and herbs and spices such as dill or ground cumin to make spicier versions. Varieties of this dip are known as raita in India and tzatziki in Greece.

1/2 cucumber, finely diced / grated

225g (8oz) Greek yoghurt

1 tsp mint, finely chopped

Salt and pepper

You will also need:
Blender

1   To remove all water, squeeze the grated cucumber gently in a tea towel, or salt diced cucumber and leave to soak for 30 minutes before rinsing and drying.

2   Mix all the ingredients together and season to taste.

3   Chill before serving.

Cucumber and yoghurt – a cool dip to complement hot curries.

Strawberry and cheese spread

225g (8oz) strawberries

225g (8oz) cream cheese

55g (2oz) blue cheese

You will also need:
Blender

Liquidise all the ingredients and use on bread or toast or as a dip.

COULIS

Coulis are thick fruit sauces or strained purées that are used to garnish desserts such as ice cream, gateaux, cheesecakes and sponge puddings. They are often drizzled across the plate in patterns and can be stirred through creamy puddings for a marbled effect. You can serve them hot or cold, so make excellent hot sauces when teamed with warm puddings such as fritters or pies.

Raspberry/strawberry coulis

200g (7oz) raspberries or strawberries, picked over and cleaned

1 tsp lemon juice

Optional:
Icing sugar, to taste

You will also need:
Blender

Fine sieve

1   Liquidise the fruit in a blender.

2   Rub through a fine sieve to remove the pips if using raspberries.

3   Add the lemon juice and, if required, sweeten with a little icing sugar.

Blackcurrant/blackberry coulis

140g (5oz) fruit

2 tbsp sugar

4 tbsp water

You will also need:
Blender

1   Cook the fruit with the water and sugar.

2   Liquidise and then sieve for a smooth coulis.

FRUIT VINEGARS

As well as creating fruit vinegars through fermentation, you can simply steep fruit such as raspberries, strawberries or blackcurrants in cider vinegar or red or white wine vinegar and use the resultant flavoured juice to create unusual salad dressings by combining it with olive oil. Fruit vinegars can also be poured over ice cream or a range of desserts, used as a marinade or treated like cordials and drunk diluted with iced water.

They are a very good way to use up over-ripe fruit that has gone a little soft and mushy, although you should certainly remove any mouldy bits first. Once made, ideally leave them for a few weeks so the flavours mature before using.

For variety, try a combination of fruit, such as redcurrant and raspberry or blackberries mixed with pear. These vinegars also make lovely Christmas presents if you decant them into miniature glass bottles.

Raspberry vinegar

900g (2lb) fruit

570ml (20fl oz / 1 pint) white wine vinegar

115-225g (4-8oz) sugar per 570ml (20fl oz / 1 pint) of juice

> ✳ As an alternative, you could add a teaspoon of good quality Balsamic vinegar to the mix before bottling, to give your vinegar a richer taste.

1. Place the fruit in a sterilised container.

2. Cover the fruit with vinegar, mash with a fork to release the juice and leave for several days, stirring occasionally.

3. Strain the vinegar. Do not press down on the fruit if you want a clear juice.

4. Add 115-225g (4-8oz) sugar according to taste and heat gently until it has dissolved. Be careful not to make the vinegar over-sweet – you can always add extra sugar when creating your dishes.

5. Boil for about 10 minutes and then cool before bottling and sealing in sterilised containers such as Kilner jars.

Blackberry vinegar

This method involves cooking the fruit in the vinegar, rather than pouring the vinegar over the raw fruit.

450g (1lb) blackberries

1 cinnamon stick

1 clove

200g (7oz) sugar

500ml (18fl oz) vinegar

You will also need:
Muslin bag

1. Hang the spices in a muslin bag in a pan.

2. Dissolve the sugar in the vinegar and then boil for 5 minutes.

3. Add the fruit and simmer for 10 minutes.

4. When cool, strain into sterilised bottles, adding a few extra whole fruit before sealing.

Chapter 12
Drinks

JUICES AND SMOOTHIES

Juices using a blender

Juices using a juicer

Cooked, unblended juices

Smoothies

CORDIALS

ALCOHOLIC DRINKS

Fruit liqueurs

Cider

Wine

JUICES AND SMOOTHIES

You can make refreshing drinks from any fruit or vegetable very easily, but for clear juices you will need to use a juice extractor, otherwise you won't be able to separate the fibre from the juice. Inexpensive models are available from about £10 and are very easy to use, as you simply feed small chunks of fruit or vegetable into the mouth of the juicer to end up with a jug of clear juice.

You should use ripe but not over-ripe, good-quality fruit or vegetables that have been well washed or scrubbed but that can include the skin and even small pips or seeds (although apple and citrus pips and thick skins may make the juice bitter, so it is better to remove these). When you have made the juice, chill and drink it within 1 or 2 days or freeze it straight away.

Smoothies are more like milkshakes, and you need to prepare the fruit for these more carefully as you will be drinking whatever you put in your blender. You can, of course, peel fruit beforehand or sieve the mixture to remove pips and seeds, but the resultant drink will still be thick and creamy.

Smoothies are made from puréed fruit often mixed with apple or orange juice and then blended with milk, yoghurt or even ice cream. Many recipes also include bananas.

Fruit lollies

Both smoothies and juices can have an extra life if you pour them into ice trays divided into sections. With the addition of sticks you will have fruity ice lollies.

Juices using a blender

When making juices this way, you will need to peel most of the ingredients and remove large seeds and stones. You can then sieve the resultant mixture to remove the smaller pips and seeds at the end. Sweeten fruit juices before or after blending with sugar or honey, or include a little naturally sweet fruit juice such as apple or orange.

Cucumber and lemon juice

1 cucumber, peeled and cubed

Juice of a lemon

Sugar, to taste

1   Blend the cucumber with a few tablespoons of water in a blender.

2   Strain the purée.

3   Add lemon juice and sugar to taste.

Tomato juice

900g-1.8kg (2-4lb) tomatoes, washed, quartered

To season:
Salt and pepper

Optional:
Sugar

Onion / garlic / celery / green peppers, chopped

1   Remove any blemishes from the tomatoes. You can also cut out the main core.

2   Simmer in a large pan for 30 minutes until soft. If necessary, add a little extra water. For variety, you can cook some onion, garlic, celery or green peppers along with the tomatoes.

3   Blend and strain the juice. For a slightly sweeter drink, return the sieved juice to the pan, add 1 or 2 tsps of sugar and cook for a few minutes.

4   Season to taste.

Green juice

1 cucumber, peeled

4 celery sticks

2 eating apples

1 lemon, peeled

55g (2oz) spinach

Blend all the ingredients together and season to taste.

Juices using a juicer

Juicing creates a clear juice, as opposed to the cloudy type that you get with a blender. The following are suggestions for vegetable and fruit juices made this way. Clean the ingredients, discarding discoloured leaves or blemishes, and then cut into chunks before passing them all through your juicer.

If there is any unpleasant scum on the juice, strain it through muslin or a fine sieve before storing or drinking.

Apple, peach and pear juice

2 apples

2 pears

1 peach, pitted

Carrot and fruit juice

3 carrots

2 eating apples

1 orange, peeled

Beetroot and carrot juice

115g (4oz) beetroot

3 carrots

30g (1oz) spinach

2 celery sticks

Plum, apple and strawberry juice

6 ripe plums, pitted

30g (1oz) strawberries

3 eating apples

2 oranges, peeled

Apple and green leaf juice

1 eating apple

30g (1oz) spinach/rocket/ watercress

140g (5oz) grapes

1 tbsp lemon juice / lime juice

Cooked, unblended juices

An alternative to blending or juicing fruit is to simmer it gently in water. This breaks down the cell walls and allows the juice to escape and, with added sugar, will result in a more concentrated juice or cordial (see page 242). This is probably a better method for extracting juice from currants or under-ripe fruit if you want to try making juice from this source.

Blackcurrant juice

200g (7oz) fruit

55g (2oz) sugar

850ml (30fl oz / 1¹/₂ pints) water

1 Simmer the fruit and sugar in 570ml (20fl oz / 1 pint) of water for a few minutes and then cook on high heat for another 5 minutes.

2 Add the rest of the water and strain the juice.

Smoothies

Although the following recipes mention a particular fruit, such as strawberries or raspberries, you can experiment by replacing these with any mix of fruit you have to hand such as redcurrants, black-berries or gooseberries. You can even add unusual ingredients such as peanut butter, chopped nuts, chocolate bars or oatmeal for something a bit different.

Sweeten sourer fruit with caster sugar, honey or fruit cordials (see pages 242-4), and if the fruit isn't ripe enough or you want to use something like rhubarb, cook it first with a little sugar. Make your drinks extra cold by crushing ice cubes placed inside a plastic bag with a heavy object and blending in the ice at the last minute. (Don't try this with whole ice cubes unless your blender is very powerful.)

You will need a blender for making smoothies.

Low-calorie blackcurrant smoothie

225g (8oz) blackcurrants

2 bananas

400ml (14fl oz) apple juice

4 tbsp low fat yoghurt

Blend all the ingredients together and serve in tall glasses.

Raspberry and orange smoothie

200g (7oz) raspberries

200ml (7fl oz) plain yoghurt

285ml (10fl oz / 1/2 pint) orange juice

1   Blend the fruit and yoghurt until smooth.

2   Add most of the orange juice and continue blending.

3   Adjust the amount of juice to give the right consistency.

Strawberry and banana smoothie

200g (7oz) strawberries plus 2-3 for decoration

2 ripe bananas

285ml (10fl oz / 1/2 pint) milk

1   Liquidise the fruit in a blender.

2   Add the milk and continue blending until it is smooth.

3   Serve decorated with sliced strawberries.

Smoothies are a great way to start the day.

Gooseberry and raspberry smoothie

100g (3 1/2 oz) gooseberries

2 tbsp water

2 tbsp sugar

100g (3 1/2 oz) raspberries

255ml (9fl oz) milk

1 Stew the gooseberries gently with the water and sugar for 10 minutes and then leave to cool.

2 Blend together the gooseberry purée and raspberries.

3 Add the milk and continue blending until smooth.

4 Sieve the smoothie if you want to remove all pips and seeds.

Rhubarb and strawberry smoothie

2 sticks of rhubarb, chopped

6 strawberries

115ml (4fl oz) apple juice

4 tbsp yoghurt

1 tbsp honey

1 Stew the rhubarb in the apple juice until tender.

2 When cool, blend with the rest of the ingredients.

CORDIALS

A cordial is a sweetened, concentrated juice that needs water or lemonade added before you can drink it. The most common ones in the shops are lemon and elderflower, but you can use any fruit – for example, a mix of apple and blackberry, or rhubarb and strawberry.

To combine sugar and fruit, either simmer the two together or make a sugar syrup and then add pre-prepared fruit juice. After cooking, you will need to collect the sweetened juice by straining the fruit mixture through muslin (just like making fruit jellies – see page 201).

When using raw fruit, or if you don't mind the cordial becoming cloudy, squeeze the fruit mixture or press with the back of a spoon to extract all the juice.

If you use sealed, sterilised bottles you can keep unopened cordials in a cool place for 1-2 months, but you do need to store them in the fridge once opened.

Blackcurrant cordial

450g (1lb) blackcurrants

255g (9oz) sugar

255ml (9fl oz) water

Optional: 2 tbsp lemon juice

You will also need: Muslin

1 Pick over the fruit and then cook with the sugar and water for about 5-10 minutes until soft.

2 Strain through muslin and stir in the lemon juice, if using.

3 Pour into hot, sterilised bottles.

Raspberry and redcurrant cordial

680g (1lb 8oz) mixed red-currants and raspberries

300g (10 1/2 oz) sugar

570ml (20fl oz / 1 pint) water

You will also need:
Muslin

1 Gently dissolve the sugar in 500ml (18fl oz) water and then boil for 2-3 minutes until syrupy. Leave to cool.

2 Mash the fruit in a bowl, add the rest of the water and then strain the mixture through muslin.

3 Mix together the fruit juice and syrup.

4 Bottle the mixture.

Apple and blackberry cordial

450g (1lb) eating apples, chopped, peeled

450g (1lb) blackberries

285ml (10fl oz / 1/2 pint) water

3 tbsp lemon juice

Sugar: 340g (12oz) to 500ml (18fl oz) fruit juice

You will also need: Muslin

1 Cook the fruit with the water for 15 minutes until soft.

2 Add the lemon juice and then strain through muslin.

3 Add sugar (proportional to the amount of fruit), slowly bring to the boil and then boil for 5 minutes. Take care not to over-boil or you might end up with fruit jelly!

4 Pour into hot, sterilised bottles.

Rhubarb and strawberry cordial

6-8 sticks rhubarb, chopped

225g (8oz) strawberries

255ml (9fl oz) water

225g (8oz) sugar

You will also need:

Muslin

1. Simmer the rhubarb, water and sugar for 5-10 minutes.
2. Add the strawberries to the pan, mash down the fruit and leave the mixture to cool.
3. Strain through muslin.
4. Pour into sterilised bottles.

ALCOHOLIC DRINKS

It is very satisfying to make your own drinks from garden produce, but if they are to be kept for any length of time and you don't want your drinks contaminated, it is very important to keep all equipment as clean as possible, or you will introduce unwanted bacteria or yeast that will taint the finished drink.

There are two different methods for making alcoholic drinks from fruit or vegetables: either add spirits to a mixture of fruit and sugar, or use yeast to produce alcohol through fermentation.

Fruit liqueurs

Although actual fruits are named in the recipes – concentrating on the most popular for home-made fruit liqueurs: blackcurrants, plums and damsons – you can substitute any soft fruit or use a mixture of different varieties. You can also experiment with different alcohols if these are more easily available – for example, use brandy or rum instead of vodka – but you should then try to use the fuller-strength versions.

Although quantities for sugar are given, this is a matter of taste. It is safer to add slightly less – you can always add a little more if the liqueur is too sharp, but can do very little about it if you have made it too sweet.

Make some plum
liqueur in time for
Christmas . . .

Plum liqueur

900g (2lb) plums, washed,
stoned and halved

450g (1lb) sugar

485ml (17fl oz) vodka

140ml (5fl oz / 1/4 pint) brandy

1 Pierce the skins and place the fruit in a large,
sterilised container.

2 Add the rest of the ingredients and stir. (Or gently
simmer the fruit with the sugar for 5 minutes first
before cooling and adding the alcohol.)

3 Seal and label.

4 Leave for several months, stirring occasionally.

5 Strain the juice, pressing the fruit to extract all the
liquid.

6 Strain again for a clear liqueur.

7 Bottle in clean, sterilised containers and leave for a
few weeks before drinking.

Blackcurrant liqueur – purée method

200g (7oz) blackcurrants

155g (5 1/2 oz) sugar

55ml (2fl oz) water

485ml (17fl oz) vodka

55ml (2fl oz) brandy

You will also need:
Blender

1 Check over the fruit and leave to steep in a hot,
sugar syrup made by completely dissolving the
sugar in hot water.

2 When cool, liquidise or mash the fruit mixture.

3 Add the vodka and brandy and decant the liquid
into sterilised bottles.

4 Store for several months and strain to remove
unwanted sediment before drinking.

Blackcurrant liqueur – whole fruit method

About 200g (7oz) black-currants – enough to two-thirds fill a container

155g (5 1/2 oz) sugar

55ml (2fl oz) brandy

485ml (17fl oz) vodka

Optional:
Spices, e.g. cinnamon stick, cloves

You will also need:
Funnel

1 Put the fruit in a glass container. Prick the berries first with a pin or alternatively squash the fruit in the container to get the juices flowing.

2 Using a funnel, cover the fruit with sugar.

3 At this stage, you could also introduce spices such as cloves or a cinnamon stick.

4 Add the brandy, then fill up the bottle with vodka.

5 Seal, label and then leave for several weeks in a cool, dark place.

6 Strain and leave for a further few weeks before drinking.

7 As an alternative, you could start with a mixture of half fruit and half vodka and leave this for several weeks before straining and adding an equal quantity of sugar syrup.

Damson and gin liqueur

450g (1lb) damsons, washed

170-200g (6-7oz) granulated sugar

1 bottle (750ml) gin

You will also need:
1-litre (1 3/4 pint) sterilised container

Funnel

1 Prick the damsons and place in a 1-litre (35fl oz / 1 3/4 pint) sterilised container.

2 Add the sugar through a funnel and then fill up the container with gin.

3 Leave for several weeks, shaking the container regularly to dissolve the sugar.

4 Test after a couple of months and, if necessary, add extra sugar.

5 After about 6 months, strain off the juice into sterilised bottles, so that the fruit cannot taint the finished drink.

6 Leave to mature for another month or so.

Cider

If you have never made cider before, you may be told that there is no need to buy special equipment. However, from my experience, you will find it very difficult without some sort of cider press: extracting juice from large quantities of apples is extremely hard work. As the presses currently on sale are very expensive, you could try making your own version: you will need a container with lots of holes, a car jack that can bear down on the apples in the container, and a tray to catch the juice. (Alternatively, look out for local charities or organisations that, for a small fee, will crush your apples for you.)

You will need sanitising powder or tablets such as Campden tablets for cleaning your equipment, and you should use airlocks on your containers to allow gases to escape without letting unwanted bacteria in. You will also need to purchase the appropriate yeast together with any recommended nutrients that help the yeast to work properly. All the equipment should be readily available from home-brewing or wine-making suppliers on the high street or online.

When making apple cider, use any fruit you have, including those a little past their best – even windfalls, as long as bad parts are cut out first and the fruit hasn't started to deteriorate. Ideally have a mix of sweet and sour apples for a rich-tasting cider. Perry normally requires special perry pears, but if you want to make some with ordinary pears try adding a few apples to increase the acid content.

The basic steps are as follows:
- Clean the fruit.
- Mash and extract all the juice.
- Add yeast to the juice to start off fermentation.
- Allow time for the fermentation process to complete.
- Decant and bottle.

Sterilise your equipment by washing containers with soapy water, then rinsing inside with a very dilute bleach solution or some vinegar, rinsing again, and finally filling with liquid made by dissolving sterilising Campden tablets in warm water. Leave this for an hour or so before rinsing thoroughly again. Put lids on your containers.

Basic cider recipe

1 Pick the fruit and, if you can, leave it to soften for a few days, although you will have to check it regularly and remove any pieces that have gone bad.

2 Wash the fruit thoroughly. Ideally wash in a light bleach solution first and then rinse well in plain water.

3 Cut up the fruit into small pieces, discarding any bad bits.

4 Use a cider press to extract as much juice as possible or, if you don't have anything like a cider press, try using a blender or juicer or pressing the pulp between boards, or simply macerate and pound the apples to a pulp.

5 Pour the mash into muslin and strain out all the juice into sterilised collecting buckets or jars.

6 Kill any residual yeast that may have been on the fruit skins by adding crushed Campden tablets to the container of juice (1 tablet per gallon / 4.5 litres) and leave it to work for a good 24 hours.

7 Now set off fermentation by adding Champagne, wine or cider yeast (plus nutrient if advised to include it) and keep the buckets or jars at room temperature. Cover and leave for 4-7 days, stirring now and again.

8 Decant or siphon it off into fresh, sterilised containers such as large glass jars or demijohns and fit an airlock.

9 Although you can allow the apple juice to ferment as it is, for a sweeter cider, add sugar, but no more than about 2lb (900g) per gallon (4.5 litres) of juice overall. Wait for a few days and then add it a little at a time dissolved in some of the extracted juice.

10 Fermentation will take about 2-4 weeks and the cider (or pear perry) should eventually be a clear liquid. Carefully decant it into sterilised drinks bottles or bags. If using glass, make sure there will be no further fermentation.

11 Store somewhere cool and try not to drink for a few months.

Wine

You can make wine from almost any fruit or vegetable, including damsons, blackberries, beetroot, marrow, rhubarb and peas, and so you may like to substitute the named ingredients in a given recipe with any surplus you have in your garden. Try to use produce that is firm and ripe, and if using root vegetables, simmer them in the water and strain the juice before continuing with the recipe.

Many vegetable-wine recipes, such as green bean, carrot and beetroot, are improved if you include chopped raisins, as these will add body. You can also add lemon juice (or citric acid) to increase acidity, as this is needed for a vigorous fermentation. Another addition is tannin (or strong tea solution), as this only occurs naturally in fruit skins. If the main fruit or vegetable constituents are high in pectin – for example, gooseberries or rhubarb – you may also need to add a pectin-destroying enzyme with the yeast (available from home-brewing suppliers) to stop the final wine becoming too cloudy.

One important part of the process when making wine is racking off. Every 2-3 months, siphon off the liquid into new containers fitted with an airlock so that you leave the sediment (lees) behind.

As it is hard to know how much sugar to add or when fermentation has ceased, you may like to use a hydrometer. This measures the specific gravity (SG), which indicates the amount of sugar still present in the 'must' (wine). When the reading steadies, it means that fermentation has finished. Many people recommend adding a final Campden tablet after fermentation has ceased, in order to kill off any stray bacteria and stabilise the wine before it is bottled.

One note of caution: As wine takes so long to mature before it is drinkable, not all of the following recipes have been fully tested! However, they give you an idea of the sort of quantities and processes involved. For more detailed advice, there are various books available on making fruit and vegetable wines at home. There are also numerous websites, including: www.howtogrow.co.uk/easy-wine-making-guide.html, www.harvington.org.uk/hic/winerecipes.html and www.thehome brewsite.org.uk/techniques/how-to-make-homemade-wine.htm.

Apple and blackberry wine is well worth waiting for.

Mixed fruit wine

2.7kg (6lb) mixed fruit, e.g. plums, blackberries and apples, washed, stoned and chopped

3 tbsp lemon juice

4.5 l (160fl oz / 8 pints) boiling water

1/2 tsp pectin-destroying enzyme

1 sachet (7g / 1/4 oz) wine yeast and nutrient

2 Campden tablets

Sugar – roughly 900g (2lb)

Optional:
1 cinnamon stick

You will also need:
Fermentation jars such as demijohns, with airlocks

1 Put all the fruit in a clean bucket together with any spices. (If you prefer, retain the fruit in a muslin bag so the pulp can be removed easily.)

2 Pour over the boiling water.

3 Add the sugar and crushed Campden tablets to kill any unwanted yeast.

4 Leave covered for 3-4 days, stirring regularly.

5 Add the enzyme, lemon juice, yeast and any yeast nutrient (follow the manufacturer's instructions).

6 Mix well and leave for a few days.

7 Now strain into sterilised containers such as demijohns. Leave room at the top for expansion and let fermentation take place slowly.

8 Rack into clean jars every 3 months to remove the sediment. Once fermentation has ceased, continue racking off until the wine is clear.

9 Bottle in suitable wine or drinks bottles and allow to mature before drinking.

✳ For a sweeter wine, you need to stop further fermentation with Campden tablets before adding extra sugar, or you will get secondary fermentation.

Courgette wine

2kg (4lb 6oz) courgettes

2 lemons

2 oranges

3 Campden tablets

1.5kg (3lb 5oz) sugar

1 sachet (7g / 1/4oz) wine yeast and nutrient

4.5l (160fl oz / 8 pints) water

You will also need:
Fermentation jars such as demijohns, with airlocks

1   Chop the courgettes and add to a sterilised container with the sliced citrus fruit.

2   Add the sugar and pour on boiling water.

3   Stir to dissolve the sugar and then add the crushed Campden tablets.

4   Leave for 24 hours and then stir in the yeast and nutrient.

5   Stir regularly for the next 4-5 days.

6   Strain into sterilised containers such as demijohns and leave to ferment for several weeks before racking off.

7   Rack off every 3 months. You should have a drinkable dry wine after about a year. For a sweeter wine, add extra sugar dissolved in a little hot, extracted wine after it has been fermenting for a few months.

Runner bean wine

1.3kg (3lb) sliced beans

4.5l (160fl oz / 8 pints) water

225g (8oz) raisins, chopped

1.1kg (2lb 8oz) sugar

2 tsp lemon juice

1 sachet (7g / 1/4oz) yeast and nutrient

1 tsp pectin-destroying enzyme

1 tsp tannin

You will also need:
Fermentation bucket

Fermentation jars such as demijohns, with airlocks

1   Simmer the beans in the water until soft and then strain the liquid.

2   Pour the hot liquid on to the raisins and sugar in a fermentation bucket and stir to dissolve the sugar.

3   Cover and leave to cool before adding the yeast, nutrient, enzyme, lemon juice and tannin.

4   Leave for a week, stirring the mixture each day.

5   Strain the liquid into fermentation jars such as demijohns and leave in a warm place until fermentation has finished. During this time, continue racking off into clean jars every month or so until the wine is completely clear.

6   Bottle and then do not drink for another few months.

INDEX